The Fibromyalgia Coach

Advance Praise

"Honest and inspiring, Tami Stackelhouse delivers a message that speaks directly to each of my patients with fibromyalgia. Her witty and empathetic tone is inviting without being intimidating and the lesson is powerful: You *can* thrive with fibromyalgia. I've seen my patients personally transformed through her coaching. They are stronger, happier, and ready to share that transformation with others."

—**Dr. Kaley Bourgeois**, Lake Oswego Health Center

"As a personal trainer and someone involved in several support groups for those with fibromyalgia and other chronic conditions, the difficulty of working comes up very often. In *The Fibromyalgia Coach*, the author shares her personal story and lots of wisdom for honestly exploring what work will mesh well with your current life and your unique personality, all while supporting you in feeling better. Included are concrete valuable steps to start pursuing a business of your own if that is a good fit for you. Unsure if starting a business is for you? This book will walk you through that exploration! The author's big heart and respect for individuality are evident throughout; making it an enjoyable, helpful, and quotable read."

—**Gillian Byers**, ACE certified Personal Trainer, MindfullyActive.com

"This book is a life changer for anyone touched by fibromyalgia! Tami Stackelhouse has successfully navigated living with fibromyalgia, and is an expert in coaching others on the topic. In *The Fibromyalgia Coach*, she outlines key questions for career exploration and re-evaluating professional success. She offers practical solutions that apply to both current and future career goals. Whether you are newly diagnosed or have been thriving for years, there is something new to learn in each chapter. The author's wisdom and personality are revealed through personal and professional anecdotes. As a clinical social worker and a person living with fibromyalgia, I have had to change my mindset and re-invent my career so that I can thrive both personally and professionally. I have used the concepts in this book to help with that journey, and Tami has been a light on my path with me."

—**Jen Shepherd**, LCSW, Founder, PainCamp.com

"As someone living with fibromyalgia, reading *The Fibromyalgia Coach* brought up a lot of emotion for me. I could relate to the author's story as she connects with readers emotionally through her personal experiences. Reading this book took me back to the time when I was in the wrong job and how my health was affected both physically and mentally. The author shows us how much our job choices affect our health and vice versa. In *The Fibromyalgia Coach,* Tami Stackelhouse has written the perfect sequel to her first book, *Take Back Your Life*."

—**Melissa Swanson**, Advocate and Author, *Ravyn's Doll: How to Explain Fibromyalgia to Your Child*, FibroWarriorsLivingLife.com

"I wish I had this book when I was recovering from Lyme disease. Lyme and Fibromyalgia are closely related; the daily pain and suffering we go through to regain dignity in our work lives is tremendous. *The Fibromyalgia Coach* offers a roadmap for getting back into the life you loved."

—**Ruschelle Khanna**, LCSW, Founder, Ascend Retreats

"Tami Stackelhouse is being the change she wants to see in the world. Better yet, she is empowering others to do the same! If you or someone you know has fibromyalgia, or if you are a medical provider, *The Fibromyalgia Coach* is a must have research and guide book!"

—**Norman F.S. Hanley**, Founder, MenWithFibromyalgia.com

"*The Fibromyalgia Coach* provides a comprehensive set of 'nuts and bolts' questions to help the reader discover both the work style and work setting that will be their best fit. The ability to find work that is compatible is one of the biggest concerns facing those of us who live with fibromyalgia. The author makes this assessment process fun by interweaving humor and lots of personal examples. Will definitely recommend."

—**Elaine Merryfield**, Fibromyalgia Educator and Author, *Life Beyond Fibromyalgia,* NavigatingLifeWithFibro.com

"This book provides practical and useful questions, ideas, and tools that will inspire fibromyalgia patients to find healing and love for their life that they may have lost."

—**Melissa Talwar**, Fibromyalgia Advocate, International Fibromyalgia Support Network

"I found *The Fibromyalgia Coach* to be very encouraging. It helps us to prioritize what is important in life when living and working with fibromyalgia. I recommend this book to people with fibromyalgia who are working or trying to find work."

—**Linda Horncastle**, Occupational Therapist

The
Fibromyalgia
Coach

Feel Better, Change Lives,
and Find Your Best Job Ever

TAMI STACKELHOUSE

NEW YORK

NASHVILLE • MELBOURNE • VANCOUVER

The Fibromyalgia Coach
Feel Better, Change Lives, and Find Your Best Job Ever

Published in New York, New York, by Morgan James Publishing in partnership with Difference Press. Morgan James is a trademark of Morgan James, LLC.
www.MorganJamesPublishing.com

The Morgan James Speakers Group can bring authors to your live event. For more information or to book an event visit The Morgan James Speakers Group at www.TheMorganJamesSpeakersGroup.com.

The advice and strategies contained herein may not be suitable for every situation. Ideas, procedures, and suggestions in this book are not intended as a substitute for consulting with your physician. All matters regarding your health require medical supervision. Neither the author nor the publisher shall be liable or responsible for any loss or damage allegedly arising from any information or suggestion in this book. The fact that an organization or website is referred to in this work as a citation and/or a potential source of further information does not mean that the author or the publisher endorses the information the organization or website may provide or recommendations it may make. Further, readers should be aware that Internet websites listed in this work may have changed or disappeared between when this work was written and when it is read.

ISBN 978-1-68350-567-9 paperback
ISBN 978-1-68350-568-6 eBook
Library of Congress Control Number: 2017906964

Cover Design by:
Rachel Lopez
www.r2cdesign.com

Interior Design by:
Bonnie Bushman
The Whole Caboodle Graphic Design

In an effort to support local communities, raise awareness and funds, Morgan James Publishing donates a percentage of all book sales for the life of each book to Habitat for Humanity Peninsula and Greater Williamsburg.

Get involved today! Visit
www.MorganJamesBuilds.com

For Debbi
who was brave enough to follow her dreams
when others would have thought it was too late.

Table of Contents

Foreword

Successful management of any chronic illness requires a large component of education on self-management skills. In an ideal world, every fibromyalgia patient's health care team would include a Fibromyalgia Coach or Advisor, along with a medical professional. Ideally these coaches and advisors will act as patient advocates, who can guide and teach other patients in self-care, what to ask their doctors, and to offer emotional support.

My patients are fortunate to have access to just such a person, Tami Stackelhouse, who is an experienced and gifted Fibromyalgia Coach. I have seen that patients working with her make progress on taming fibromyalgia symptoms much faster. I can give medical advice, like suggesting someone avoid gluten, or eat more protein, or perform gentle exercise. The hard part—for all of us!—lies in executing those changes. That's where I've seen my patients improve with Tami's help. She has also helped them add joy back into their lives. Shifting your mindset, even a little bit, can result in a huge transformation. In her newest book, *The Fibromyalgia Coach,* Tami continues her message of hope that you can thrive, help others, and feel fulfilled even with a fibromyalgia diagnosis.

This reminds me of the first patient I diagnosed with diabetes. As I launched into my eager young doctor two-minute spiel about the importance of exercise and diet changes to manage diabetes, the patient stared back at me stunned, like a deer caught in headlights. I quickly realized she needed a lot more education on this subject than I had the time or expertise to offer. Since changing behaviors is difficult, she would also need advice, moral support, and encouragement.

Thankfully, for the newly diagnosed diabetic, there are nurse educators who do exactly that. I referred my patient to one, and when she returned for a follow-up appointment, she was confident and making positive changes in her life. I was blown away by the difference that a few hours of education and coaching could make.

Fibromyalgia desperately needs a similar model. According to The American Pain Society guidelines, "patient education is critical to optimal management of fibromyalgia." Currently, however, fibromyalgia education is left to the individual provider who has scant time and sometimes little knowledge about what to teach or how to teach it effectively. Nearly half of all primary care doctors reported uncertainty diagnosing, treating, and managing patients with fibromyalgia.

Fibromyalgia Coaches and Advisors fill this critical gap in the health care system, by giving clients up-to-date information on current research and treatment options and helping them navigate effectively through a confusing health care landscape and prepare for doctor appointments. This is especially vital for patients living in places where they just don't have adequate medical resources or specialists. Coaches and advisors teach their clients how to exercise the right way, make dietary changes that can reduce pain, and best track symptoms to monitor treatment effectiveness—things challenging to figure out on your own, especially when you're bogged down by fog, pain, and fatigue! Coaches and advisors can be fibromyalgia patients or health coaches who have undergone specialized fibromyalgia training; they don't necessarily need to be nurses or health care professionals.

I hope one day it will be as common for doctors to refer their patients to a Fibromyalgia Coach or Advisor as it is to refer to a diabetes nurse educator. And since there is only one Tami, I am thrilled that she has founded the International Fibromyalgia Coaching Institute to train others to be Fibromyalgia Coaches and Advisors.

Ginevra Liptan, MD
Medical Director, The Frida Center for Fibromyalgia
Author, *The FibroManual: A Complete Fibromyalgia Treatment Guide for You and Your Doctor*
Portland, Oregon

Introduction

I became a Fibromyalgia Coach by accident. My path could have gone thousands of different directions. You'll read about some of those in this book. There were two major crossroads, without which I wouldn't be here and you wouldn't be reading this book.

- I never intended on developing fibromyalgia. Who does?
- When I decided to become a coach, I told my husband we would have to do it together. He promised that he would do a lot of the work since I was so sick. I laugh about that now because he doesn't coach at all. Still, that promise was enough to get me in the door.

Like all good stories, where I started isn't where I finished. The Great Storyteller only tells redemption stories—and this is the story of how my fibromyalgia and becoming a coach not only gave me a better life, but also made me a better person and changed the world around me.

Let me start off by describing a little of what we deal with as fibromyalgia patients.

Fibromyalgia is more common than you think.

According to the National Fibromyalgia & Chronic Pain Association, two to four percent of the world's population has been diagnosed with fibromyalgia; 80 percent of those diagnosed are women.[1] Using this statistic and a conservative estimate of three percent, this means that one out of every 21 women in the United States is currently diagnosed with fibromyalgia. I've heard some estimates as high as six to eight percent of the population and the male to female ratio of diagnosis as high as 40 percent men, 60 percent women.

I think there are some simple reasons why it's hard to know for sure how many people have fibromyalgia. It takes several years and many doctors to finally arrive at an accurate diagnosis. It also takes many of us a long time to realize that something is wrong. In my case, I thought everyone was tired and hurt like that—even in their 20s. (How wrong I was!) In the case of men with fibromyalgia, there's the whole image of being the "tough guy," "men don't cry," and being the provider of the family that makes it tough to admit you're exhausted and in pain. Then, there's our society, which seems to award bonus points if you can function on a few hours of sleep and a lot of caffeine!

The result is the same—a lot of hurting people.

The United Nations estimated that there would be 7.3 billion people in the world by August 2016. Using that three percent statistic again, that could mean at least *219 million people* suffering from this one chronic pain illness: fibromyalgia.

There aren't enough doctors.

Fibromyalgia currently falls under the heading of rheumatology, even though recent studies seem to indicate that it's more of a central nervous system disorder than a rheumatological concern. This "disease without a home" situation can make it a real challenge to find doctors who understand fibromyalgia. A study published by *Arthritis & Rheumatism*, the journal of the American College of Rheumatology (ACR), says, "smaller micropolitan areas of the U.S.—those with less than 50,000 people—have very few or no practicing adult rheumatologists. In some of these areas, individuals have to travel more than 200 miles to reach the closest rheumatologist."[2] Traveling several hours to see your doctor—one way!—is pretty impossible when you're living with chronic pain and fatigue.

Even in larger cities, there is a real shortage of rheumatologists and doctors who know how to treat pain. A 2005 ACR workforce study estimated that for every 100,000 people there were 1.7 adult rheumatologists.[3] Using our same average of three percent of the population being diagnosed with fibromyalgia, that equals 1.7 rheumatologists for every 3,000 fibromyalgia patients—assuming those rheumatologists saw no other kinds of patients! The statistics for chronic pain patients in general are even worse. There are at least 100 million people in pain and at most only 4,700 pain specialists.[4] That's more than

21,000 patients per pain specialist. While all those numbers are mathematically correct, they just "don't add up." It simply isn't possible for one doctor to see 3,000 fibromyalgia patients or 21,000 pain patients![5]

Doctors don't have enough time.

In the 2010 National Ambulatory Medical Care Survey (NAMCS), over half of all doctor visits are 15 minutes or less; almost 90% are less than 30 minutes.[6] When I was researching information for my first book, I also ran across this information found in Kaiser Health News:

"A 1999 study of 29 family physician practices found that doctors let patients speak for only 23 seconds before redirecting them; only one in four patients got to finish their statement. A University of South Carolina study in 2001 found primary care patients were interrupted after 12 seconds, if not by the health care provider then by a beeper or a knock on the door."[7]

When you have an illness like fibromyalgia, it can be impossible to get all your questions answered in 15 minutes, especially if you're interrupted after a few seconds!

In the physicians' defense, it's difficult for them too. They just don't have an hour a week to spend helping one patient understand how to change her diet or manage his energy. Doctors don't have time, or often the know-how, to help their patients figure out why they didn't meet their goals that week or go to bed on time. If the doctor doesn't have fibromyalgia personally, they don't understand our pain or fatigue either—or why "simple" goals are hard for us to accomplish.

Work isn't designed to help you get better.

In case you haven't noticed, your boss at work isn't focused on reducing your fibromyalgia symptoms. They're probably more focused on the bottom line, right? I know I'm not the only one who can look back at my career and clearly see where workplace chronic stress led to my development of fibromyalgia.

What can you do?

My goal in this book is to help you clearly define what you need physically, mentally, and socially—in life, not just in a job. I also want you to know the best way for *you* to measure success. Once you discover these things, you will be able create a fibro-friendly career that is perfect *for you*. A job that meets all your needs, and helps you feel better instead of leaving you feeling stuck, tired, hurting, and stressed out. I'll also outline for you some of the obstacles you'll likely face, as well as how to plan your way around them. Most importantly, I'll tell you about the full-time job you already have that will pay you massive returns on any investment. Finally, for those of you who are curious, I'll explain what a Fibromyalgia Coach is—and why being one has improved my own fibromyalgia symptoms.

Are you ready? Great! Let's go….

Chapter 1

Is This You?

*"I have a feeling that my job is the thing
that is holding me back from getting better."*
—Melanie

I had been working with Melanie for about six months when she was laid off from the job she loved. After her initial fear, she was relieved. It meant that she would have the opportunity to focus on feeling better. After a couple of months off, her fibromyalgia improved and she found a new job. A few weeks later, during one of our coaching calls, I asked her how the new job was going. "Oh my goodness!" she said. "I love it but the people here have *so much energy!*" She went on to explain that everyone was a bit younger than she was and very active. A common occurrence for her was to be talking with someone as they walked to the conference room. Instead of riding the elevator, like she needed to, her co-workers would head right up the stairs. It put her in the awkward position of making a big deal out of not taking the stairs—which, of course, brought up all kinds of things about how much to say about her fibromyalgia, especially at a new job. Most of the time, she chose to stay quiet, take the stairs, and pay for it later in the day. I wasn't at all surprised when she told me, "I have a feeling that my job is the thing that is holding me back from getting better."

I don't know what kind of job you have right now, but I do know fibromyalgia. If you're working a traditional office job, you're likely triggered by the fluorescent lights, sounds, hard floors, uncomfortable chairs, or using your computer all day. If you're lucky enough to work from home, I know it's still that: *work*. There are deadlines, schedules, difficult customers to deal with, and so on. If you're a stay-at-home mom, you probably have the hardest job of all; your work literally never ends and there are no days off!

As an employee, the thing that I hated most was someone else dictating my schedule. I felt like I was still in high school and needed a hall pass to go to the bathroom or leave campus for a doctor's appointment—except that I was in my 30s! To me, there is nothing more demeaning than having to ask permission to take care of yourself. It's also a good way to end up skipping the self-care we need, simply because we don't want to go through the hassle.

Portland had a massive snow storm one year that came between two ice storms. On my street, there was an inch of ice, covered by several inches of snow, topped off by another thick layer of ice. I walked out to my car to test and see if there was any chance of me driving to work the next day. First, my foot slipped on the top of the ice, then it cracked through and sunk into the snow. Just when I thought I'd made it, I almost fell on my butt because my foot slipped on the final thick ice layer at the bottom. Nope. Totally not driving!

I live on a private gated street, so there were no snow plows and no way for me to go to work. I also live on the side of a pretty steep hill. All of Portland was dealing with the same weather, but I had to call in and explain to my boss why I couldn't be there. I still remember that "getting called to the principal's office" feeling of dread as I prepared to make that call. The following morning, I made the same call; as you might imagine, that snow and ice hadn't magically vanished overnight. I was told that my boss would drive over and pick me up. All the news channels were saying, "Don't drive unless you absolutely need to." The mayor even released a public safety notice asking people to stay off the streets. In my opinion, driving to the office to help someone with their software doesn't qualify as an emergency. It wasn't like anyone was going to die if we weren't there. Not to mention the fact that some of our work—like returning customer phone calls—could have been done from the safety of our own homes. I felt unsafe walking the block from my house to the corner where he could pick me up. I felt unsafe riding in the car with him to the office. I was unable to have anything like a lunch break that day since there was no way for me to get away from the office. I felt like I was being held hostage by my boss. At the end of the day, there was the ride back home on those same unsafe streets. I couldn't quit because I was single and had just bought my house. I was the only income earner; I was too scared to leave. At the same time, I vowed that I would *never ever* allow myself to be in that position again.

You have probably been in that position before as well. Maybe it wasn't because of a snow storm. Maybe you just needed to see your doctor, or go to physical therapy. When you have fibromyalgia, it takes more… let's call it *maintenance*… than someone else might need. When I was first diagnosed with fibromyalgia, I was seeing my doctor every three weeks as we tried different medications and therapies to find the combination that worked—and that was just my primary care appointments. My doctor also wanted me to see a physical therapist a couple times a week, and have massage and acupuncture once a week. That's a full-time job just seeing providers! I work with many of my clients on prioritizing their care so that they can get the treatment they need without setting themselves back. Kind of silly, isn't it? You schedule so many doctor appointments, trying to get better, that it *causes* a fibro-flare! When going to those appointments requires you to have someone's permission or possibly schedule all those appointments after working all day, it's just not realistic.

Then there are the bad days. The fibromyalgia flare days.

For many of my clients, calling in sick to work feels like lying when it's "just" because they're so exhausted they can't get out of bed or hurt too much. Especially when they sound fine on the phone. It's not lying, but it often feels like it. Even if you feel confident in saying you're sick when it's pain or fatigue, you might feel like your boss doesn't believe you.

Have you missed so much work that you've felt like your job was in jeopardy? Or decided not to work or volunteer because you feel your health is so unpredictable? Have you considered that maybe your best option is filing for disability... yet you feel like you aren't actually, you know... *disabled?*

The lack of flexibility in the work-world makes it difficult for those of us who have unpredictable illnesses. Deep down, you're probably feeling like if you could just find the *right job* or the *right boss,* you would probably have a lot to offer. If you could just find a boss who was understanding, an office that was physically comfortable, and a schedule that was flexible enough to support you. If you could set up your own work hours, doing work that made you feel good physically and emotionally, you could keep working even with fibromyalgia.

Right now, you probably feel like you must choose one or the other: you can work OR have a life. You don't get to have both. You suspect that if you didn't work, you might have the energy to do things like travel with your family or play with your kids and grandkids. You could volunteer for causes you are passionate about, go shopping, cook for your family, say yes when friends invite you to something, or whatever it is you can't do right now. You can get through a work day now. You show up even though you're hurting and exhausted. You haul yourself out of bed, even when you feel like you could sleep for a week, and you ignore the stabbing pains as you sit at your desk. When you get home, you collapse on the couch and feel guilty that your kids are having to take care of you instead of you taking care of them. Which leaves you feeling like you shouldn't apply for disability because someone who's disabled can't work at all, right? Sound familiar?

Maybe you've already started thinking about how you can reduce your work hours or change your schedule to work around your fibromyalgia. Maybe you are hoping that you can work from home a few days a week, or start later, or work shorter hours. You think that these things might be the answer, but you're afraid that if you tell your boss why you need these accommodations, it might put your job at risk. You're afraid that instead of being supportive of your needs, your company will use it to replace you with someone stronger, with more stamina, and with fewer issues. Yes, firing you because of your illness is illegal. However, if you can no longer fulfill the requirements of your job, they are within their rights to find someone who can. In addition, many states, like Oregon for instance, have a "no fault" rule, which means you can be fired at any time for any reason. I used to do the hiring and firing for my department. There are ways to do this legally, such as if you are late to work too many times, or miss too many days of work without the protection of the Family Medical Leave Act (FMLA).

You've probably also started to feel like all your thoughts and decisions are revolving around the f-word. (That's "fibromyalgia," in case you didn't catch that!) Your whole life begins to center around taking your pills and supplements at the right time, scheduling doctor appointments, and avoiding things that will cause you pain. It becomes a never-ending saga of saying no and taking things away. Your doctor tells you to stop eating sugar and gluten. You can't meet your friends for coffee because you're too tired. You can't meet them for pedicures because the scrubbing and buffing hurts too much. You say no to your kids because you're tired. You say no to your husband because you have a headache (and you really do). You feel like your whole life has been consumed by the monster that is fibromyalgia, your body has betrayed you, and all that's left of your life is scraps. Even if you've done a lot of work and your fibromyalgia has improved, you're still tired of always having to do the work: taking the pills, watching your diet, managing your energy. You're starting to lose your motivation and just want a break.

Does any of this resonate?

I want you to know that your intuition is right on. The work you do and the job you have can make all the difference in your fibromyalgia journey. Your job truly may be the thing that's holding you back from getting better. The good news is that I believe there's a perfect career out there for you. This book will help you find something that you love to do that not only makes space for, but increases, your healing. For me, it's being a Fibromyalgia Coach. Throughout this book, I'll obviously be using that as my example of the perfect career because it is my perfect career! However, the key questions I give you will be useful to help you discover the career that's right for you—even if it's doing something else. I want you to find what is right *for you*. Maybe it's doing the kind of work I do, maybe not. That's totally okay. At the end of the book, I simply want you to be clear on what is best for YOU.

Chapter 2

My Story

"You can do anything, but not everything."
—David Allen

*"It's only by saying 'no' that you can concentrate
on the things that are really important."*
—Steve Jobs

A s I said in the introduction, I became a Fibromyalgia
Coach by accident. I was one of those kids who was
good at many things; I was told often that I could be
anything I wanted to be. Well, when you can be *anything*, it's
hard to choose. The options are quite overwhelming.

The earliest memory I have of a career choice was wanting
to be a librarian. I *loved* my books! I had a bookshelf in my

room that I would organize and reorganize over and over. I would put books in alphabetical order. Then, I'd rearrange them and put them in order by subject matter. I received book plates as a gift and put them in all my books, just like the library does, to show that they were mine. I couldn't imagine a job more wonderful than being surrounded by books every day. I even made my little sister come check out books from my library.

Then, in third grade, I decided I wanted to be a paleontologist—I even learned how to spell "paleontologist" *as a third grader.* This was inspired, in part, by a stegosaurus named George. I'd even had an imaginary pet tyrannosaurus rex for years when I was younger. In case you are wondering, in my mind's eye, Rex was basically a giant head. Let me tell you, as a shy kid there was great comfort in knowing that the biggest monster wasn't under my bed, he was my best friend! Unfortunately, I learned that being a paleontologist meant doing hard work in dry, dusty places. It also often meant things like scorpions. Sorry, no dice. Nope. Not for me after all!

In high school, I decided that I wanted to be an astrophysicist… until I realized all the classes that I would have to take before I could get to "the good stuff." I called those classes "Styrofoam." I didn't want to chew through years and years of Styrofoam to get to the real meal. As a default choice, I followed a friend to college and majored in music. I'd taken piano lessons for 10 years, and loved to sing, so why not? When I got there, I found more Styrofoam—and, I believe, some of my first signs of fibromyalgia. I had a hard time getting up for classes. I couldn't eat on a schedule that helped me feel my best.

Most importantly, living in the dorm, I could *never* get away from school! That left me feeling overwhelmed, drained, and nearly raw from too much stimulation. I went back home after just six weeks as a freshman.

I spent the next year taking care of myself. It was one of the best years of my life. I started reading books on health and discovered holistic medicine. One of my favorite things that I learned from that year is that the word "holistic" has the same root as holy, whole, healthy, and hale. I learned that to be healthy meant to also be whole, holy, and holistic. I took an hour walk every day in the country, down to an old bridge crossing a small creek. I would listen to radio shows I had recorded on my tape recorder as I walked. (This was back in the early 90s, before the days when you could subscribe to podcasts!) Those recordings were from theologians, motivational speakers, and other self-improvement lecturers. I got in touch with who I was, and more importantly, who I was made to be.

After a year of filling myself up with all this goodness—good food, fresh air, healthy movement, and all these juicy words—I went back to college. This time, I majored in Fashion Merchandising and Interior Design. I loved *all* those classes. No Styrofoam there! After a year and a half, I decided to consider transferring to a design school in downtown Portland. That's when the Styrofoam showed up again. The classes were fun and *amazing*. However, I learned that the actual work that designers do is often spent alone. I didn't relish the idea of working in an office by myself; I was massively disappointed. I ended up dropping out of college because it seemed like a lot of money to spend when I had no idea what I wanted to do.

I had a friend who lived an hour south of me who worked at Hollywood Video, a video rental store. His store was hiring, so I applied, got the job, and moved. I spent the next two years working at the store. This was one of the first major video rental stores in the town at the time, so *everyone* came to our store. We even had the governor of Oregon come in, along with her bodyguards. After two years of that job, I realized that I could talk to *anyone, anywhere, anytime.* This was a huge thing for a girl who grew up as the shyest person in her class! I thank God for Hollywood Video because today I talk to people for a living.

Renting videos is a fun job when you're in your early 20s, but there isn't much room for greatness there. In my soul, I know I was made to do and be so much more. Therefore, when a former co-worker showed up looking more fabulous than ever, I wanted to know what she was doing. Turns out she had become a Mary Kay consultant and was teaching people about skin care and makeup. I was intrigued. After all, I had been a fashion merchandising major. Going to my first Mary Kay event opened my eyes to the fact that there were people who dreamed of changing the world. They talked about the ways that skin care and makeup could truly change a woman's life. I fully believed this from my own experiences. When I felt beautiful, I also felt confident and powerful—like I could change the world. After becoming a consultant, my favorite classes were with teenagers, teaching them how to take good care of their skin and wear makeup properly. I loved seeing their faces light up when they looked in the mirror—or hearing the excitement in their voices when they would report back to me months later that they felt confident and beautiful in their own skin.

Eventually, I moved back to Portland. Through my Mary Kay connections, I started working at a software company as a Customer Service Representative (CSR). I loved my work! I loved talking with people all over the world, helping them solve problems in creative ways. It wasn't just about how to use our software. For me, it was about teaching them how to use our software to help them accomplish their goals, build their businesses, and change the lives of their clients. I also learned about what I call "the question behind the question." I discovered that many times when a customer called us, the question they asked wasn't really the question they needed answered. For instance, they might call and ask, "How do I run this report?" What they truly wanted to know, however, was how to find out if a certain product was profitable, or if a certain person was a good referral partner, or even, simply, how much money they'd made that week. Often, the report they were asking for wasn't the best way to get the information they wanted. Working as a CSR helped me hone my listening skills and how to get to the "question behind the question" through asking questions of my own. I also became comfortable talking on the phone. It's what I did 40 hours a week. This may seem like nothing to you, but when I was a teenager, I was so shy that I wouldn't even call my best friend on the phone. I would wait for her to call me.

I also became an excellent teacher. I taught our customers over the phone how to use their computer and our software. ("Click here. See that little box on the right corner of your screen? Click there." And so on.) After I became the Customer Service Manager, I did the hiring and firing for my department. I trained new and existing employees, and traveled around the world training our customers in person. I wrote the instruction book for my staff on how to walk a customer through correcting different software errors, upgrades, database repairs, and so on.

I worked at that company for nearly 10 years. As the Customer Service Manager, I managed the call center and email tech support staff, and coordinated all our customer training events. As you might imagine, it was often stressful. People don't usually call tech support just to say they love your product! If the phone rang, it was because someone had a problem. Every day was a cacophony of sounds: phones ringing, keyboards clacking, voices talking. More than once I had customers yell at or be rude to me. If someone did that to my staff, the call was forwarded to me to handle. Don't get me wrong, most of our customers were kind and generous. I even had one customer who called me every Friday afternoon, just so I could teach her one new thing that week. Still, the constant stress took a toll on me. I believe this is why I developed fibromyalgia.

I remember one day when I was in my 30s, sitting in my office. I had been searching for years for answers to why I was always so tired and why I hurt every night when I got home. As I sat in my office chair at my desk, I remember being mind-numbingly exhausted. I distinctly remember thinking, "If I could just close my office door, turn off the lights, and lay down on the floor, I would be asleep in two seconds!" Man, I wanted to! I ended up making a coffee run instead, trying to prop myself up on caffeine and sugar. My days went on and on like that until eventually my body just couldn't do it any longer.

In May of 2006, I married Scott. After just two months of seeing how that job affected me, he told me to quit. Whether it was because I no longer had to be strong, or because I had the space and support to let go, my health began to collapse. Despite the growing pain, fatigue, and brain fog, I kept trying to work. After all, that's what you're supposed to do, right? I didn't have my fibromyalgia diagnosis yet, so I think part of me thought that I just needed time to recover from the stress of being a manager.

I started working as a virtual assistant creating newsletters. Every month, I would take my clients' sales reports and put them into a newsletter template that they could print and mail to their people. I thought, "This will be great! I can work when I want, rest when I want, stay at home, and give myself time to recover." Well, not so much. You see, their sales reports wouldn't be available until the 5th of the month, but my first round of newsletters were due on the 10th. At one point, I had around 100 clients who all needed their newsletters between the 10th and the 25th of the month. 100 newsletters in two weeks. That's a lot of work. While I could do it when I wanted during the day, I still had to get it all done during a certain time of the month—regardless of whether I was having a good day or a bad day. It became harder and harder to do my work. I hurt sitting in front of the computer for as long as I needed to in order to get things done with that quick of a turn-around. I would sit at my computer for hours on end, not taking a break, because I thought it would help me get things done faster. I stayed up late into the night... until one day my husband pointed out that the later I stayed up, the more often I'd be saying things like, "Dang it!" "What the heck?" "Why isn't this working?" "ARGH!" <smile> Apparently, it wasn't my computer that didn't function well after 10 PM. It was ME. Huh.

I was diagnosed with fibromyalgia during this time, and so many things started to make more sense—the brain fog, body pain, fatigue, and why I wasn't recovering from stress or illnesses as quickly as I wanted to. I started to cut back on the number of newsletters I did every month because it was just *so hard*. Other virtual assistants I knew made more money than I did because they could take on more clients, and here I was needing to work with less. Ultimately, I made an error that got me fired. Looking back, I can see exactly why it happened. I wasn't thinking clearly and made some bad decisions. It was truly an innocent mistake, but it was HUGE, and it cost me all my clients.

At that point, I had no job and questioned my ability to be able to work at all. I had made such a grievous error that I honestly didn't trust myself. Then I discovered something important.

I already had a full-time job. My job was to heal.

Chapter 3

Healing Is a Full-time Job

"There is no escape. You have a full-time job;
you are always at the office of healing."
—**Kris Carr**, from the trailer for her movie, *Crazy Sexy Cancer*

W hen you have a chronic illness, as Kris Carr says, there is no escape. That's the definition of chronic: "persisting for a long time or constantly recurring." It means that there are no days off and no vacations. Many fibromyalgia patients tell me, "I'm so tired of thinking about my illness all the time. I'm sick of my life revolving around what I can and can't do!" I absolutely get it.

My husband has a 1991 Harley-Davidson Heritage Softail. The first few years after we were married, some neighbors would come see us every so often to talk motorcycles. They were part of a group at their church that would get together on weekends and ride. Every month, Scott and I were invited to go on one of these rides with them. I wanted to—I mean really, a *church motorcycle club?* If nothing else, I wanted to check that out! Unfortunately, we always turned them down because I hurt too much, or was too tired, or didn't think I had the stamina to go for the whole day. Eventually, they stopped asking. Years later, when my fibromyalgia had improved to the point I felt like I could go on one of those rides, we asked them if they were still meeting. The group had stopped riding together and we missed out on the opportunity.

Maybe there are things in your own life that you've missed out on like that. Maybe you've said no so many times that your friends have stopped asking—or even stopped being friends. Maybe you missed out on opportunities with your children or grandchildren. Maybe you missed business or travel opportunities. All because you were so focused on your illness and how it was limiting your life.

I want you to know that there is hope.

Just like losing weight, training for a marathon, or learning to be a great pianist, you may have to give up some things *temporarily* to get something better later. I believe that fibromyalgia gives us that opportunity.

When I was fired from my virtual assistant job, I realized that I had a massive opportunity in front of me. Instead of getting stuck feeling sorry for myself for what I did wrong and losing my job, I could focus on all the extra time I now had to get well. I decided that I wasn't going to feel useless, worthless, or depressed because I was "lying around doing nothing all day."

Instead, I was going to make it my full-time job to get well. To heal my fibromyalgia as much as possible and become as healthy as I could be. I didn't run across Kris Carr's quote until many years later, but it so perfectly captures what I decided that day: I have a full-time job. I am always at the office of healing. *And I love my job!*

If you want to learn the ins and outs of what I did to get well, I suggest reading my first book, *Take Back Your Life*: *Find Hope and Freedom from Fibromyalgia Symptoms and Pain.* In that book, I outline the basic things I did to reduce my pain, increase my energy, and get better sleep. I also talk about the lessons I learned in how to work best with my doctors, what I could do to help myself, and how working with a coach changed the whole game. Getting out of my super-stressful software career was just the tip of the iceberg. There was a *lot* of work I did, in many areas—and sometimes that hard work looked exactly like rest. Finding a career that supported that work has meant that I can stay feeling good. Today, I don't have many fibromyalgia symptoms. When I take care of myself the way I need to, I have zero body pain and enough energy to do the things I want to do. My brain functions like it used to and I sleep well at night.

As you begin to think about the career that will support your own health and healing, I want you to make one fundamental shift in your thinking.

Your world doesn't revolve around your illness.
It revolves around your healing.

I get why people don't want to think about illness all the time. It's depressing, limiting, and can even feel hopeless. When you think in terms of healing, however, that opens the door to possibility, options, and my favorite—hope.

There is a huge difference, mentally, emotionally, and spiritually, between saying, "I can't go because of my fibromyalgia" and "I choose to stay home so that I can feel better." From the outside, it may not look any different; you're still staying home. However, by making the *choice*, you are opening the door for something better. You are opening the door for healing.

Is that a new thought for you? This isn't just woo-woo stuff I'm talking about here. It's actually physically, scientifically, different.

First of all, our brain has this thing called the reticular activating system (RAS). It's a system that helps you recognize more of what you're looking for. Have you ever bought a new car, one you thought was fairly unique, only to drive it off the lot and start seeing cars like it *everywhere?* That's your RAS in action. You can "program" your RAS to find more of what you want by focusing on what you want. You decide you really want a little red sports car and start seeing red sports cars everywhere. You decide that black and white polka dots are cute, and you start seeing them in every store window. This is how I stumbled across using cherry blossoms as my logo, like on the cover of this book. I started seeing them everywhere. My RAS was kicked into gear and showed me cherry blossoms *everywhere.* I finally had to go look up what they meant in Japanese and Chinese art to understand what my RAS was trying to tell me.

When you sign up to receive the bonus items that come with this book, you'll receive my article, "Cherry Blossoms as a Symbol for Fibromyalgia," which will have more details. The nutshell version is this: in both cultures, cherry blossoms are a symbol for femininity. Since my focus is on helping women with fibromyalgia, this is appropriate. In Japanese art, a cherry blossom on the ground symbolizes a life cut short—something that many of us feel has happened when our illness changed our lives. They also symbolize the delicate and transitory nature of life. I believe this is an excellent message for those of us who are living with fibromyalgia. Good days and bad days come and go. Many times, we feel delicate, almost fragile—physically, mentally, emotionally. Even our spirituality can be affected. With all these changes, it can be helpful to realize that "this too shall pass."

In Chinese artwork, however, cherry blossoms are a symbol of strength and femininity.

I decided I wanted to use both the Japanese and the Chinese symbolism. I want to take my clients from being a "Japanese cherry blossom" (someone who is delicate, fragile, and feels as if her life has been cut short) to being a "Chinese cherry blossom" (feminine, strong, and in control of her own life). Just visit FibromyalgiaCoachingInstitute.com/book-bonuses to sign up and receive the full article.

With our health, it works like this: if you focus on what you can't do, your RAS will find more of what you can't do. If you focus on opportunities to heal, your RAS will find you more opportunities to heal. It's almost like magic. If you're interested in learning more about the RAS, search YouTube and you will find some videos that explain it well.

Another factor is selective attention: our ability to focus on something that is going on while other, non-related things are going on at the same time. You might read that and think that with fibromyalgia you don't have any selective attention. Not true. Go look online for "The Monkey Business Illusion." I won't give away what happens in this video, because if you don't know, the first time you see it, it's pretty stunning.

The point is that a lot of opportunities might be around you and you're simply not seeing them. By changing your focus from illness to healing, you will get your brain to start showing you those opportunities.

Interestingly, the effects of stress can also be reduced simply by knowing that the stress response is there to help us. This is your fight or flight response, which fibromyalgia patients tend to get stuck in. Kelly McGonigal discusses this in her TED talk titled, "How to Make Stress Your Friend." She mentions a study that looked at the effects of stress on 30,000 adults over the course of eight years. The people who believed that stress was bad for your health had a 43% increased risk of dying. Here's what's fascinating:

"People who experienced a lot of stress but did not view stress as harmful were no more likely to die. In fact, they had the lowest risk of dying of anyone in the study, including people who had relatively little stress. Now the researchers estimated that over the eight years they were tracking deaths, 182,000 Americans died prematurely, not from stress, but from the belief that stress is bad for you."[8]

I think this is even more applicable to those of us with fibromyalgia because the stress response is so involved in our illness.

Knowing all of that, can you see why choosing to make healing my full-time job, instead of not working because I couldn't, allowed me to heal even faster? If you're having trouble with this mental shift, please visit FibromyalgiaCoachingInstitute.com. On the site, you can connect to one of my amazing Certified Fibromyalgia Coaches or Advisors to help you with this work. It can often be difficult to do this on your own, especially if it's something new and foreign to you. Having someone to hold your hand and guide you through the process can make it go more smoothly and quickly. The more quickly you make the shift from focusing on your illness to focusing on healing, the more quickly you can get back to living the life you want to live.

If you want a little reminder to keep you focused on your healing, visit FibromyalgiaCoachingInstitute.com/book-bonuses to download a "Healing is a full-time job" mantra coloring page created especially for readers of this book by artist Anne Manera. You can also find her coloring book *Fibromyalgia Mantras: A Coloring Book for Fibro Warriors & Chronic Pain Heroes* on Amazon or on her website at AnneManera.com.

Imagine no longer being held prisoner in your own body. No more being held hostage by the doctor who prescribes your medications. No more being a victim of a broken medical system. Focus on your healing—and get help from a coach if necessary—and you'll be the one in control. No one else. Not even your illness.

Chapter 4

Discover Your Physical Needs

> *"Being alive is a gift. Nurturing your*
> *body is just a way to say thank you."*
> **—Lissa Rankin**, MD

I n this chapter, I will be giving you four different questions to ask yourself as you evaluate your physical needs. Don't worry if you don't know the answers to these questions right away. If you find yourself in that position, you can begin by simply paying attention. After you read these questions, start paying attention to what helps you feel better and what makes you feel worse. As you notice new things, make a note of them. It may be helpful to use a journal dedicated to these reflections; an app on your smartphone could also work. If you'd like, I have a few worksheets on my website that you can download and print to help you through this process. You'll find the "Getting to Know You" worksheet and "Career Evaluation Form" at FibromyalgiaCoachingInstitute.com/book-bonuses.

How much control will I have over work hours and deadlines?

I used to always say that if I was going to see a sunrise, I'd have to stay up to do it. I've always been a night owl, and have never been a morning person. I now know that some of that is a result of my inverted cortisol levels, something very common in fibromyalgia patients.

When I was in my 20s, my best friend marveled that I had seemed to find the perfect job for me when I was hired at Hollywood Video. I generally worked from 4 PM to midnight during the week and 6 PM to 2 AM on the weekends. In my 30s, however, I had a typical office job and worked 9 AM to 5:30 PM. Getting to work by 9 AM was nearly an impossible task. I think that was listed as an "area to improve" on all my employee reviews!

When I decided to try working for myself, having control over my work hours was the number one thing on my list. I wanted to be able to work when it felt good, and when I was functioning at my best. This was about two things for me: 1) how I felt and 2) doing good work. When I don't get enough sleep—or don't sleep during the right hours—I feel terrible. When I shift too far from my natural sleep/wake cycle, my fibromyalgia is worse, my brain fog is paralyzing, and my pain increases. It always ends up taking me so much longer to do the work I need to do when I feel like that. In addition, my work during those times is generally filled with more errors, is less creative, and, frankly, not as good. I can't problem-solve as well. I have trouble finding the right words. I start spelling things funny and can't do simple math. All of that means that I don't feel as confident or capable. I feel stupid. Slow. Ineffective. Who wants that?

Now that I'm my own boss, I get to choose when I work. My current work hours are from 10 AM to 6 PM. I never hold an appointment before 10 AM, if I can help it. I know that trying to coach someone when my problem-solving skills aren't top-notch isn't good for them or for me! As you consider the kind of work you want to do, consider how much control you'll have over those work hours. Can you work during your best hours? Or are you on someone else's schedule?

As I mentioned in my story earlier, I have held many kinds of jobs. Even working as a virtual assistant and as an independent Mary Kay consultant, I didn't have as much control over my hours as I expected. When I worked as a virtual assistant, I could work any time of the day or night. That part was easy. Getting all those newsletters done in such a tight turnaround was hard. Depending on how the dates fell, I might have just a couple days to do their newsletters! Sure, I could work after 10 AM, but in those two days I might work 20 hours or more. Having to do all that work, under pressure, with clients emailing me anxious for their work to be done, was highly stressful. Sure, I got it all done in those two days, but I put myself in a fibro flare to do it. Those 20 hours of work cost me several days of recovery time… just in time to do it all over again.

Then there are the bad days. What happens if you have a bad day—or a bad week or more? As you're looking at your options, be honest about how often this comes up for you. How many bad days do you typically have in a month? Is there a pattern for when they occur? For many people, Mondays are bad days because they've overextended themselves on the weekend. I know that was true for me! Even now, I plan for my Monday to be an administrative day so that I have time to ease back into my week.

When I started my coaching practice, I was concerned about having bad days. Therefore, I decided to do all my coaching over the phone. I knew that even if I had to coach from my bed, I would still be capable of having a phone conversation. I also knew that if my clients were having a bad day, they would be able to have a conversation too. I didn't want my clients to ever feel like they had to cancel an appointment because they were in a flare—that's when they would need me most! I also knew that if I was working with people who have the same illness as I do, if I absolutely could not function, they would understand. After all, they've been there themselves. I've also learned how to schedule my coaching calls so that I have the time I need during and between calls to be kind to my body. I have time to get up, stretch, not be at the computer or on the phone too long, have a snack, do some meditation, or pet my cat. (Okay, that often happens during coaching calls! I love my SamSam's Belly of Happiness and Joy!)

As you're looking at the flexibility of your work hours, also consider if you might occasionally want to work more or less. Maybe there are certain times of the year that you're more prone to be in a fibromyalgia flare. Or maybe you want the flexibility to work more and earn extra money occasionally. My sister, Debbi, was diagnosed in March 2016 with stage IV gallbladder cancer. She passed away in June after only a three-month battle. I will forever be grateful that I could work less during those three months so I could be with her as much as possible. I will never be able to get back that time with her. It makes losing her so much easier knowing that I have no regrets about how my time was spent from the time she was diagnosed to when she left us. I'm also super grateful to have had the time to mourn, recover, and plan a magnificent Celebration of Life memorial service for her. An employer, even the most understanding one, wouldn't be able to give me six months off. Nor could they allow me to decide moment-to-moment whether I would work or go visit my sister. But I could—and did.

Another thing that was crucial for me was no longer having to ask permission to take time off. I was tired of feeling like a kid in school who had to have a hall pass to go to the bathroom. I'm an adult who should be trusted to make good decisions about what I need to do to take care of myself *and* get my work done. It was beyond frustrating to me to have to save all my personal leave days in case I got sick or needed to go to the doctor (or acupuncturist, or yoga, or physical therapy, or massage, or....). For many years, I really didn't take vacations because all my personal leave days were spent on the appointments I needed to keep myself functional. As you might imagine, no vacations didn't exactly help my health either.

Do you feel like you're stuck in a situation where you must ask permission for everything? Are you frustrated, feeling like you have to share too much of your personal life—and your health—in order to justify the time off you need? In order to do the physical therapy your doctor has recommended, do you have to have an unwanted conversation with your boss about your illness, explaining that your doctor has prescribed this? Have you ever had to get a doctor's note for time off? Sucks, doesn't it?

When I left my last job, I swore to myself I would *never* be in that position again. There is so much freedom in being able to do what you need to do when you need to do it— without having to justify it to someone else first. It is my heartfelt wish for you to have this freedom yourself. It will improve your fibromyalgia symptoms in so many ways. You will have less stress, calming down the overactive "fight or flight" response we have as fibromyalgia patients. You will be able to take care of yourself in the ways you need to in order to feel your best. You'll be happier not having to justify *every little thing*. In my experience, happier generally means less pain.

What equipment or skill set is needed?

As you're thinking about finding a fibro-friendly career, spend some time thinking about what skills and equipment you have and enjoy using.

I often hear my clients contemplate being a virtual assistant. I think this is the number one job consideration when someone begins to think about working from home. The reality is, if you don't like computers, or using one causes physical pain, this could be worse than your current career!

Be honest with yourself about how you feel doing different kinds of jobs. Be sure to evaluate how you feel physically, emotionally, and spiritually. Maybe talking on the phone drains you. Maybe it makes you feel great because of the social connection. Perhaps it only works for you if you have a headset and aren't holding a phone to your ear. Maybe video is okay. Maybe video stresses you out because of the technology or feeling like you always want to look your best. Perhaps you have a bad shoulder or carpal tunnel and can only use the computer for 20 minutes at a time. Maybe you need to alternate between standing and sitting, or prefer to be moving around. Maybe the only comfortable place you have during the day is on your bed, or in a favorite recliner. Whatever it is, be honest about what you *really* need to feel your best.

Depending on the job, you may need to consider purchasing equipment. Here are a few examples:

- Software (This can be a biggie, as some software, like that used for photo or document editing, can be expensive and may require a different kind of license if you're using it for business purposes.)
- Dedicated phone or fax line
- High-speed Internet connection
- Webcam
- Phone headset
- Printer or scanner
- Stand/sit desk
- Ergonomic chair or keyboard
- Special orthopedic shoes for standing or walking

- Storage space for inventory or supplies
- Office space
- Locking file cabinet (Depending on the type of work, this may be a legal requirement.)

Think also about the skills you have and the skills you might need to learn. If you want to be a virtual assistant, you might need to brush up on your computer or technology skills. If you want to be a coach like I am, you might need to learn how to do that. As I'm interviewing applicants for my training program, I look for people who are already skilled in communication and compassion. These are the people who are natural coaches. If you were the person your friends always came to for advice or for a shoulder to lean on, then you would probably make a great coach.

Don't think you need to know everything before you start. That used to be me. I remember once signing up for a dance class with my sister. I think it was a swing dancing class. Deb was a natural dancer and could pick up a whole dance routine by watching someone else do it once. I, on the other hand, was totally terrified. I remember saying to her, "I just wish I could learn the steps before we go." She, of course, laughed and said, "You'll learn them when we get there. This is a *dance class.* You do know that's what it's for, right? To learn?" I felt a little silly after that because she was totally right. Everyone would be learning the steps with me. It's not like I was going to the class to perform like a star. I was going to *learn.* In the same way, I don't expect my students to know everything about fibromyalgia and coaching before they take my class. That's what the class is for.

To learn, practice, discover what you're good at, and who you work with best. If you think you might want to be a graphic designer, take a class at your community college. If you want to be a virtual assistant, consider interviewing one about what their business is like. If you're thinking that you might want to be a Certified Fibromyalgia Coach or Advisor, and this book doesn't answer all your questions, reach out to me. I'm happy to tell you more.

One more thing on equipment and skills: don't discount your own personal preferences! You will *always* be better at the things you like to do. My sister was so good at picking up dance steps because she absolutely loved dancing. I am so comfortable on the telephone that I can have a conversation with someone as effectively as if I was there in person. Talking to and working with people is so natural to me that I almost can't *not* do it. Think about the things you'd do *even if nobody paid you.* That's where your magic lies. Tap into that and it will be more like playing than it is like work. I promise.

What is the volume of work?
I talked earlier about the flexibility of working more—or less— if you need to. In order to know if you'll have that kind of flexibility, you'll need to know the potential volume of work. If there isn't a lot of potential for work, then it will be difficult to work more and earn more when you need to.

In the case of Fibromyalgia Coaching, I'm often asked if there's a "market" for that. Many people think that the focus is too narrow and it would be hard to find clients. That's absolutely not the case.

In the Introduction to this book, I talked about some statistics. Two to four percent of the world's population is diagnosed with fibromyalgia. That is as many as 19 million people just in the United States who could use a Fibromyalgia Coach. I certainly can't help all those people myself. As a coach, I usually worked with 10-20 clients at a time in one-on-one sessions. To reach all those fibromyalgia patients, we would need one to two million coaches and advisors—just in the United States alone. There's a lot of work to be done. I feel a real sense of urgency to help these hurting men and women—but not at the expense of my own health. In honoring my own boundaries, I must find other people who want to help me with this work. I can't do it alone, and there is plenty of work to go around.

Whatever you are considering doing, be sure to look at the volume of work available. Is it enough to get you the income you're needing? Is it so much that it would cause you a flare when trying to handle it all?

In my training program, I require my students to complete the Dream Week Planner exercise from the chapter on energy in my book, *Take Back Your Life*. To receive their certification, I must approve their dream week. The reason I do this is because I want them to think through how much work they want to do, when their best working hours are, and plan for their self-care and family time. Most importantly, I want them to create a business plan that is sustainable, realistic, nurturing, and profitable. It doesn't help clients—or make you any money—if you work so hard that you put yourself into a flare.

I love being able to control how much—or how little—I work. As I mentioned earlier, I reduced my work hours to spend more time with my sister during her cancer treatment, and took even more time off when she went on hospice.

I also have the flexibility to make more money by going out and finding more work. For example, my husband works for a large corporation. In 2016, they had several rounds of layoffs and furloughs (where the company is closed and nobody gets paid). There were many times that his paycheck was cut in half due to the furlough. There were also many times we weren't sure if he was still going to have a job at the end of the day.

It has meant so much to me to know that I will never be in that position. I am 100% responsible for the money I make—or don't make. Yes, that means that I must find my own clients. More importantly, however, it means that I can't be laid off or have my paycheck cut.

You may be thinking that my income is based on what my clients do or don't do. It's normal to have clients discontinue working with me for various reasons. Most often, it's because they have learned all they need from me so that they can manage their fibromyalgia on their own. By tracking my business, I know that on average, clients work with me for 27 weeks, or about six months. Think of any professional you've seen for your illness (doctor, acupuncturist, massage therapist, chiropractor, physical therapist, and so on). I'm sure that at some point, you stopped seeing most of them for one reason or another. Maybe money was tight, or you found someone closer to home. Maybe it became difficult to get the appointment times you wanted, or you just fell out of the habit. Maybe you even felt that you'd gotten all you could from that provider and needed a fresh perspective. Coaching is no different. When you know it's going to happen, you can plan for it.

The most common question I'm asked in student application interviews is if fibromyalgia patients can afford to pay for coaching. The common perception is that those suffering from fibromyalgia aren't working, or are living on disability income. There is some truth to this, but it's not the complete picture.

The results of an Internet survey of over 2,500 people with fibromyalgia was published in 2007 by a group of four universities and the National Fibromyalgia Association. They discovered that half of the survey responders worked and half couldn't. The research article states, "The respondents were nearly equally divided regarding their ability to maintain gainful employment." They also found that, "Approximately 20%... had filed some form of disability claim and 6% received workman's compensation." In terms of income, the survey results showed over 20% had a household income over $80,000. Using the same statistics I used earlier, this means that there are 3.8 million fibromyalgia patients with a household income over $80,000. Over 10% (1.9 million) have a six-figure household income.[9]

I also think it's important to connect with patients *before* they are no longer able to work. Think about your own situation. You probably started feeling symptoms long before you received your diagnosis. If you don't work now, I'm certain there was a time between when you were diagnosed and when you had to quit working. What if you had found the help you needed during that time and had been able to keep earning an income? Most of the time, we hide our fibromyalgia. We don't tell friends or co-workers that we're struggling. We barely even admit how we're feeling to our doctors. People with fibromyalgia who are "highly functional" aren't obvious to the outside world. They go through the day and crash when they get home, or on weekends. Their families might know that something is wrong, but not know what exactly it is. Oftentimes, things don't become obvious until their symptoms are so bad that they can no longer work.

Let me ask you this: What would it be worth to you to find a way to keep working and stay productive? What would it be worth to not feel the way you do right now? To be there for your kids and your family? To keep your active lifestyle and social activities? To contribute to your family's income? What *have you already paid* in terms of doctor visits, therapies, pills, and supplements? Did you ever buy something off an infomercial in the middle of the night because you were willing to try something—*anything*—that might work? (I certainly have!) Have you done anything that your friends and family thought was crazy, like throw out all your belongings and move somewhere new because mold might be increasing your symptoms? Have you left friends and family to move to a new climate—warmer or cooler—and hoped it would ease your symptoms? If you added up everything you have spent, even if insurance covered some of it, what would the cost be? What would the non-monetary cost be in things like friendships lost, family arguments, financial stress, and the loss of your identity? It adds up, doesn't it? A study published in the January 2011 issue of the *American Journal of Physical Medicine & Rehabilitation* found that the direct medical costs for fibromyalgia patients is double that of non-fibromyalgia patients. In this study, it was a difference of about $2,000 per year.[10]

This is what I believe we offer as coaches. Our clients may still need to pay for doctors and treatments, but we can guide them into the treatments and providers that will be the most effective for them, saving them money in the long run. We also help them manage their symptoms and live the life they want to live. It's like those old MasterCard commercials. There might be a cost for coaching, but what you get in return is something priceless: your life back.

All that to say, there are plenty of fibromyalgia patients who can afford coaching.

If you want to work with those who can't afford coaching, there are ways to do that as well. You can sponsor a fibromyalgia support group, coach a certain number of pro bono (free) clients, or offer a scholarship to clients in financial need. There is absolutely a way to make an income coaching while still having a heart of service. In fact, I think it's crucial to keep a heart of service. My first book, *Take Back Your Life,* is an example of how I do this. In my book, I give you the same things that I teach my students and clients— and I probably give away more copies than I sell! I also have many articles on my personal blog, offer free webinars, speak at events, and give away my knowledge in many ways. If you want to be on my mailing list to receive notices when I offer these free events, visit FibromyalgiaCoachingInstitute. com or follow me on social media. You'll find me under "FibroCoach."

Another way I can control my income is by knowing my business numbers. I know how many people I need to talk to in order to gain one client. I know how to network and build relationships with providers to get referrals. I know the results of my advertising efforts—what is effective and what isn't. I know everything I need to do to have a steady stream of clients—which means I can predict my income and business so that I can adjust as needed.

If you decide to work for yourself—no matter what kind of work it is—you'll want to research the market and know what kind of work is available. You'll also want to track your business numbers so that you can have stability and confidence. Knowing how much potential work is available is important, but so is knowing how you are performing at that work.

How physically demanding is the work?
It's crucial that you truly know the physical demands of the work you're considering. When I decided to try being a virtual assistant, I was honestly surprised by how physically difficult that job was. It was hard sitting in one place that long, staring at a computer screen. As a coach, I need to watch out for that same trap! I am careful to schedule my calls in such a way that I get the physical breaks I need. I also use a headset so that I'm not holding my phone to my ear for an hour at a time.

Think about *all* aspects of the job, not just the "delivery" portion. For instance, maybe selling crafts on Etsy seems simple enough... until your hands are cramping because you can't knit or bead any longer. Selling things on eBay might seem like an option... until you realize you need to drive in traffic to take boxes to the post office or set up equipment to take good photos. As a Mary Kay consultant, the skin care classes and parties were easy to do, but I had heavy bags that I had to carry in and out of my clients' houses with my supplies.

If you're not sure how demanding a job might be, reach out to someone who is doing what you want to do and ask. People are often willing to do "informational interviews" for others who are considering doing the work they do. This is why I decided to start training coaches. Prior to founding the Institute, I received an email or two a month from people saying, "How did you become a Fibromyalgia Coach? What training did you get? I'm thinking it might be a good option for me. How do I do this too?" I was always happy to talk to those people—remember there are more people with fibromyalgia than I can help on my own! If I hadn't had those conversations, the International Fibromyalgia Coaching Institute wouldn't have been born.

Action Steps

I want you to spend time thinking not only about what you *can* do but what you *want* to do. Don't start from a place of lack (what you can no longer do). Start from a place of possibility. Dream a little. What would the perfect job look like physically? How much work do you want to do? Do you want to work consistently or have periods of work and rest? I have created a simple worksheet that gives you space to think through each of these questions and write down what you need and want. Don't forget to check in with your body, mind, and spirit as you do this. Your body is talking to you. She knows what she needs from you. Listen to her. Maybe she's saying, "I really need to be able to sleep in! If we can start work at 10 AM, I promise we can do great things together." That's what my body told me and I'm so glad I listened!

I also recommend checking in with those who know you well. Often, they will notice things that you won't. They may have a better idea of what makes you feel better or worse because they notice when you're happy or grumpy! They might notice when your face is pinched from pain or you walk differently because you're tired. Many times, they are also better at identifying your strengths and what you're naturally good at. I also suggest asking your doctor and other providers what they suggest. They might have good recommendations on what will support your healing and reduce your triggers. For example, your physical or occupational therapist can give tips on setting your office up more ergonomically. Your doctor might give you guidelines for how many hours you should work, and so on.

As always, the first step is awareness. Start paying attention and make notes as you think of things. As I mentioned earlier, you can find the "Getting to Know You" worksheet and "Career Evaluation Form" on the Institute website with prompts to help you think through some of this. Visit FibromyalgiaCoachingInstitute.com/book-bonuses to download these free resources.

Chapter 5

Discover Your Mental & Social Needs

"Stop trying to 'fix' yourself, you're not broken. You are perfectly imperfect and powerful beyond measure."
– Steve Maraboli

Back when I was still seeking a diagnosis, trying to figure out what was wrong with me, I remember sitting in my chair in my office feeling so exhausted. I remember looking at my computer screen and thinking that I didn't even have enough energy to *think*. Just trying to form a complete thought was almost too much effort, much less trying to problem-solve or be creative. Not only does fibromyalgia cause extreme fatigue, but it causes lots of cognitive issues as well. One study compared the "attentional blink" between people diagnosed with fibromyalgia and those diagnosed with ADHD.[11] It's not surprising to me at all that there were similarities.

There are a lot of things that you can do to decrease your brain fog symptoms. Some are habits that you can create so you don't have to remember, such as always putting your keys in the same place when you come home. Other improvements can be made through medication, supplements, brain training, and more. Getting better sleep, reducing your fatigue, and lowering your pain levels will also help you think better. If you're looking for ways to improve how your brain functions, reach out to one of my Certified Fibromyalgia Coaches or Advisors for a consultation. They know lots of tricks and tips for you. Visit FibromyalgiaCoachingInstitute.com to find the perfect coach or advisor for you.

You will want to consider your level of "fibro brain" as you're looking for your perfect career path. You will naturally be better at some tasks than others. Maybe you're great with words, but totally suck at math—or vice versa. Having fibromyalgia only accentuates the good and the bad. As I hope you can tell, I'm quite comfortable with words. This is my second book, after all! But I can always tell when it's time for me to take a break because I will start spelling things phonetically instead of the way they should be spelled. (Example: if I'm having a fibro fog moment, I would have spelled that "fonetic" instead of "phonetic".)

There are two main questions to ask yourself to assess the mental/emotional realm when considering a fibro-friendly career. Let's look at each of them below:

How mentally and emotionally demanding is the work?

As I said above, certain things will always be harder or easier for you, even if you're operating at 100%. Both the good and the bad will be amplified with fibro fog. You want to start with what you're good at.

Start by identifying your personal strengths in the mental and emotional arena. Once you've done that, you can start comparing your strengths to what is required in the career you're considering. I was already good with a computer before fibromyalgia. I ran the support department of a software company in my old life. I managed the call center, which included all the email support. This meant that doing computer-y things after developing fibromyalgia was still easy for me. Mentally speaking, working on the computer as a virtual assistant was no problem. The problem only came in when I took into consideration the questions from the last chapter—the volume of the work and the cramped deadlines. That much work in so few days maxed out my brain power. It meant that simple things became difficult—like answering my husband when he'd ask me what I wanted for dinner. I had nothing left in my brain! During the time I worked as a virtual assistant, I didn't read many books, even for fun, because my brain was all used up. This from a girl who used to check out—and read—three books a day from my school library.

As a coach, I have a practice that allows for "on" and "off" times for my brain. I describe this in more detail in my first book in the chapter on energy, including the pattern of work I use during the week to allow both my brain and my body to rest. Within each day, I also have a pattern of work and rest that I follow. An average coaching call is 45-60 minutes. After each call, I have a 30-minute break (or longer) before the next coaching call. During that break, I complete any follow-up tasks, such as emailing resources we talked about during the call and completing call notes (particularly if the client is filing for disability and may need my testimony). When I finish those tasks, I have nothing outstanding for that client. This allows me to completely "close the book," so to speak, and not have anything hanging over my head. I don't have anything to remember, because it's either noted down in my call notes or already completed. (When I am interrupted and can't follow that process, sure, I forget stuff with the best of them! That's why I have a routine and process that I follow religiously with every single call.) After my tasks are completed, my brain can fully relax for the rest of my break. I can get a snack, get up and stretch, go to the bathroom, check out Facebook, and love the cat—and my husband too, if he happens to be taking a work break at the same time. This leaves me ready to fully engage when it's time for the next client.

I also structure my day so that I'm using my brain during the times it works best. I talked in the last chapter about the fact that my work day doesn't start until 10 AM. Trust me, you wouldn't get the same level of coaching from me at 6 AM, so it's in my clients' best interests. As I teach my students about this, I have them consider what this may mean for the time zones they'll be working in. For me, working from 10 AM to 6 PM Pacific time means that I can't coach clients on the east coast who want to work in the mornings. 10 AM my time is already 1 PM their time. However, it does mean that I can work with clients until 9 PM Eastern time. With the hours that you work best, and the time zone that you're in, who can you work with best? Some of my graduates work with moms who have fibromyalgia. Others are fantastic with young adults who are working full-time. Those two coaches have different working hours and styles due to the differences in their ideal clients' lives. In the last chapter, I told you about having my students create their own Dream Week Planner. I also have them create an ideal client profile. By putting these two things together, we can find the perfect fit for each new coach in terms of what hours they function the best plus the hours that their clients will need them. If you'd like to download a copy of a blank planning sheet, and get a video walking you through filling out your own Dream Week Planner, visit FibromyalgiaCoachingInstitute.com/book-bonuses. I also describe the step-by-step process in *Take Back Your Life* in the chapter titled, "How Can I Have More Energy?"

For me, working with clients is mentally energizing. I love solving problems and puzzles. I do things like play Sudoku and complete nonograms for fun. Helping a client figure out how to have more energy or decrease her pain is another puzzle for me. It's mentally stimulating with the emotional reward of being able to make a difference in that person's quality of life.

What gets you excited? What makes you more mentally alert and awake? Are you like me and enjoy puzzles? Do you like organizing and optimizing things? Do you like making things pretty? Do you need to be creative? Those are all clues as to what might be the perfect career for you.

How social is the work?

Are you an introvert or an extrovert? Or are you an ambivert and somewhere in the middle? For an introvert, working with people can be very draining. If you're an introvert who is already tired and fogged over from fibromyalgia, you will want to be careful of how much people time you have. On the other hand, if you're an extrovert, you will want to be proactive about making sure you get *enough* people time. Fibromyalgia can be very isolating. I have a client who is very much an extrovert. She found herself getting depressed because she was tired, in pain, and often had to cancel events with friends. We focused on how she could satisfy her extrovert's desire to be around people while still managing her energy and pain. Getting enough people time made her much happier—and as I said earlier, happier usually means lower pain levels.

When I was in high school, I wanted to be an astrophysicist. I loved science and space. I read things like Einstein's Theory of Relativity… *for fun.* Then, one day out of the blue, I had a vision of myself. I was in a white lab coat in an all-white room. There were no people around; I was alone. I realized that I needed to be around people and changed direction. Now I talk to people every day for a living.

Here's the thing: you can be social without having to be somewhere physically. In today's day and age, we are meeting virtually more and more. There are conference calls, webinars, and video calls. We connect with people online almost constantly. If you're an extrovert and people energize you, there is no shortage of ways to get your people fix. In her commencement speech at our spring 2016 graduation, Jessica Gimeno of Fashionably

Ill talked about the importance of community. As one of her illustrations, she told us about her virtual New Year's Eve party. Every year, she hosts an online party where chronically ill patients can join in to watch a *Twilight Zone* marathon, share pictures of themselves in their party clothes, and even have a virtual holiday potluck by posting pictures online of what they were eating—*all without leaving their homes.* Jessica's blog is fantastic; you can find her at JessicaGimeno.com.

Coaching from home has been the perfect way for me to get just the right amount of people interaction. I get to choose who I work with and when I work with them. There are no energy vampires sucking the mental and emotional life out of me. If I find myself on overload from too much people interaction, I can dial it back and change up my schedule to have fewer coaching calls.

You'll also want to consider if you're best with people one-on-one, or if you prefer working in groups. Of course, with coaching, you can go either way. I work with clients one-on-one and run my mentorship and training programs as groups. I like both for different reasons. As a Mary Kay consultant, I mostly did skin care classes or parties—usually three to five people at a time. Working as a virtual assistant, I had very little client interaction. Most of my time was spent working alone in my office on my computer. I'd get emails from my clients once or twice a month, letting me know what they needed me to do, but I never talked to them on the phone.

Which do you like best? How do you like to communicate? Do you like email, phone, or video? Would you prefer to work with people in person? Graduates of my training program get to choose how they run their coaching businesses. Some of them work like I do—over the phone. Others are doing live video calls. Still others are teaching classes and running support group meetings in person. The beauty is that when you are the boss you can make your business your own and work the way you want to work. Certain types of businesses lend themselves to different types of social interactions, however, so it's important to think this question through fully. It's like me being a scientist in a white room. The science was compelling and sexy… but being alone wasn't. Funny thing—I had the same thing happen when I decided in college that I wanted to be an interior designer. Fortunately, I went to a design school near me and talked with them about what being an interior designer meant. I learned that only a small portion of time was spent meeting with people. There also wasn't as much time spent shopping as I hoped. <grin> Most of an interior designer's time is spent working alone on plans and design schemes. Me, alone again—only perhaps in a more colorful room!

Action Steps

Start paying attention to the times you feel energized and excited. Are you with people? How many people and for how long? Do certain kinds of people make you feel good, while other personalities drain you? Do you enjoy solving puzzles? Do you light up when you're being creative or making something more beautiful? Do you get excited about systems and organization?

The best place to start is always with awareness. Learn what makes you tick. Discover what you need to be at your mental and emotional best. Pay attention to your natural rhythms. Listen to your body as she responds to different stimuli and situations. She will clue you in on what will help you feel your best.

As in the last chapter, once you know what's best for you, compare that to the career you're considering. Does it match up? Use your discernment to discover if you will be able to create the environment you need to feel your best and do your best work.

Chapter 6

Measuring Success

*"Never doubt that a small group of thoughtful,
committed citizens can change the world;
indeed, it's the only thing that ever has."*
– Margaret Mead

When I quit my full-time job and filed for disability due to my fibromyalgia, I was often flooded with feelings of uselessness. Before my illness, I considered myself very successful. I was working full-time, making good money, and was the third person in line for running the company. I had a brand-new car and had bought a brand-new built-just-for-me house. I married a great guy, had my dream wedding, and an awesome honeymoon. Then, I crashed. Two months after Scott and I were married, I quit my job. About six months later, I was diagnosed with fibromyalgia. A year after that, I was filing for disability. As crazy as it seems, we sort of "forgot" that we were down to one income and kept spending as if we had two for the first six months or so. Then we started getting the medical bills. Finances were crazy and I could barely get out of bed. I couldn't clean the house. I couldn't cook dinner. I couldn't even be a "stay at home wife" because I physically couldn't do those things. It sucked feeling like I wasn't contributing to our little family in *any* way.

I am one of those people who is a born encourager and supporter. I was just made that way. To be in a position where I needed to be the one receiving encouragement and support was difficult. I was also smart and very self-sufficient before fibromyalgia. Scott and I were married a few weeks after my 35th birthday. That meant lots of years of doing well and handling it all on my own. Thank you very much. And now? Ugh.

I hear this same story over and over from my students and clients. Here are a couple quotes from applications I've received from those interested in joining my training program:

> *"I have been on leave from my teaching job I loved. Not long into my career, I became ill. I now have no source of income. I'm heartbroken and want to make a difference again like I was when I was teaching."*

> *"I thought, before fibromyalgia changed everything, that I was on path to making a difference. I met with committees, wrote legislators, and helped with fundraising*

for various groups and causes that I was invested with. I fed hungry children. Fibromyalgia brought all that to a halt for me."

"I am fighting every day to decide a major in school because this pain takes so much from me. I feel as if I am being robbed of my life and missing my kids' lives too."

I'm sure you're no different. You probably feel like you want to be making a difference and contribution to the world, as well. Fibromyalgia might have taken a lot from you, but you don't feel, you know… *disabled.* You still have gifts to offer, love to give, and dreams to live, don't you? Fibromyalgia doesn't have to take those away from you. There are lots of things you can do to still feel successful and fulfilled.

Let's explore the two key questions to ask when deciding if the work you're doing will meet your definition of success.

Am I getting a good return on my investment of time, money, and energy?

Most of the time when people talk about getting a good return on their investment (ROI) they're talking about money. You absolutely should consider how long it will take you to make back the money you've invested in your new adventure.

All of this is true for those of us with fibromyalgia, but there's so much more for us to consider when we calculate our ROI. When you have fibromyalgia, *everything* costs you. Sometimes it costs money. Other times, it costs you time and energy that you can't get back. It may also cost you pain or a bad night's sleep. It may cost you being able to be with the people you love or do the things you enjoy most. I don't know about you, but I feel like life is meant for *living,* not just for *making a living.* Spending all my energy on simply making enough to pay the bills, but not being able to enjoy my life, is not a good return on investment.

In my first book, I talk about the term "flareworthy." This term is used to describe those activities that are worth doing, even if they put you in a fibromyalgia flare. This term came up in my support group when one of our members was talking about taking an all-day painting class. She absolutely hurt when it was over—and hurt for a few days—but said it was "flareworthy" because it filled her with so much joy.

Is your work flareworthy? If you go into a flare for a couple days because of the work you did, would you think it was worth it?

When I was a virtual assistant creating newsletters, I was paid $10 for the 20 minutes it should have taken me to do a newsletter. In theory, I was making $30 per hour. For me, however, there were a couple catches:

1. Thanks to fibro brain, it took me more like 30-40 minutes. That brought me down to $15-20 per hour.
2. All the extra hours and hard work at the beginning of the month meant that I was in a flare for a week (or more) after the work was done. Each day of work cost me one day of recovery, which brought me down to $10 or less per hour. AND I couldn't live the life I wanted to live on my days off because they were all

spent recovering from work... just to go back and do it all over again.

I had all the skills and equipment needed when I began working as a virtual assistant, so I had zero financial investment. However, my time and energy investment was massive with negative returns.

At the time I'm writing this in 2017, Oregon's minimum wage is right around $10 per hour. If you work a minimum wage job for four hours a day, then lose an additional four hours to recover from working hard, your hourly wage is really only $5 per hour. Think about what you're giving up for those dollars. Are you paying your bills but missing out on your kids' lives, or the travel you thought you'd be doing in your retirement, or even just a pedicure date with the girls? There may be a better way that doesn't cost you quite so much.

When I became a coach, I did make a financial investment. I took classes, went to conferences, and trained to receive my health coach certification (two of them, actually). I also hired a coach myself so that I would understand the value of coaching. (Personally, I would never hire a coach who didn't have a coach of their own!) Over the years, I've spent more money on being a great coach than I ever earned as a virtual assistant. At the same time, I've received so much more back. Yes, I make good money—but what's so much more important to me are the lives that I'm changing. To quote one of my students who became a Certified Fibromyalgia Advisor after spending many years on disability, "I always thought I'd spend the rest of my life in my recliner. Now, I can *make money* from my recliner!" She also happens to be amazing with her clients and I frequently have people request to work with her. Last fall, another of my coaches posted a testimonial from one of her clients on Facebook. Diane said, "Terry is the only person in my life who understands my pain, fatigue, and depression. If it wasn't for her I think I would give up." Seeing this literally made me tear up because if I hadn't started doing the work I do, Terry might not be doing the work she's doing, and Diane may have given up.

Which leads me directly to the second question to explore when measuring success…

Am I making a difference?

I don't know about you, but I want to leave the world a better place than when I entered it. I don't want to just get up, eat, work, eat, sleep, and eventually die. I want to make a difference in the world around me. I want to help other fibromyalgia patients have hope and find the healing I've found. I want to increase the quality of life of those around me.

What are your dreams? What kind of difference do you want to make in the world?

As I mentioned earlier in this book, my sister passed away in June 2016 after a three-month battle with cancer. She was in her second year of veterinary medicine at Oregon State University. In addition to all her school work, she volunteered at Pro-Bone-O, a clinic that provides free veterinary care for the pets of people who are homeless. (Find them online at ProBoneO.org.) Our family was contacted by the clinic after Debbi passed away to let us know that they had planned to present Deb with an award and never had the chance to tell her or do so. At her Celebration of Life memorial service, we got to see the plaque with her listed as the first recipient of the award. They even named the annual award they will give to future volunteers after her. It's the Debbi Bricco Service Award. What makes me happiest about this is that the award was inspired by her life, not her death. What kind of life are you living—and what kind of work are you doing—that might inspire people to honor you?

When getting ready to write my first book, I did an exercise where I thought about what would happen if I *didn't* write my book. My list was long, especially when I focused on how your life might be the same or different. Without my book, readers might turn to people like their doctor, a counselor, or perhaps a support group. However, they might also turn to alcohol or drugs (prescription or otherwise) to try to dull the physical and emotional pain. Then, I got to the last item on my list… If I didn't write my book, there would probably be someone, somewhere, who may commit suicide because she couldn't handle the pain any longer, who couldn't find any more hope. Depending on how mild your fibromyalgia is, you might find this an exaggeration. Let me give you an actual quote from a woman I coached. This is what she said at the beginning of our first phone call:

> *"I have no idea who to turn to for help and feel very abandoned. It has been hard for me to find understanding practitioners who understand that young people can have chronic pain too. If this is what my life is going to be*

*like...." She paused for a long moment. "I don't want to
live like this."*

When we got to the end of the call, she said this:

*"I have to say how incredibly grateful I am already to have
someone to talk to for support and who understands."*

I have occasionally received emails from people who say
that they had given up, were considering "ending it all" (some
actually use that phrase), and that finding me and my book gave
them hope again. Talk about making a difference!

As a Mary Kay consultant, I found it fascinating how skin
care and makeup could change a woman's life. When you feel
pretty, you also feel more confident. Helping someone change
from having skin they wanted to hide from the world to feeling
pretty and confident was very rewarding. When I worked as
a virtual assistant, I didn't have that same kind of emotional
reward. Yes, my clients appreciated the work I did for them.
It made their lives easier... but I don't know that it made the
world a better place.

As a Fibromyalgia Coach, I literally change the world every
day, one person and one conversation at a time. It's given me
a platform to seek social change. As I write this, Oregon is the
only state in the US that doesn't cover treatment for fibromyalgia
on their state health plan. If you have fibromyalgia and are on
the Oregon Health Plan (our Medicaid program), *you cannot
receive treatment for your fibromyalgia.* I have been fighting this
battle since 2013, testifying before committees, writing articles,

working with local doctors and researchers, and even talking about this on a national and global stage—like here in this book.

The patients I talk to are often terrified of the changes they're seeing in the health care and insurance fields—especially with all the changes and stigma surrounding pain medications. All too often, patients are having what is working for them (their pain medication) pulled out from underneath them. Drug stores can now refuse to fill prescriptions your doctors have written. If this hasn't happened to you, you might think that surely there was a mistake. I assure you there was not. I have received many messages from panicked pain patients who don't know what to do.

This is an excerpt of a Facebook message I just received yesterday from a patient who was having her treatment plan cut with no warning:

> *"I'm very upset about this as I need [my medication] to work in order to live with less pain."*

She went on to talk about the fact that before she found her doctor and received the correct dose of the correct medication, she was unable to work. Once her pain was adequately managed, she could work again. It's a very frightening thing to realize that you may be going back to the "dark ages" of your life. To quote Dr. Lynn Webster, author of *The Painful Truth,* "We don't have a problem with pain medication. We have a problem with *pain.*"

What are you passionate about? Are there social injustices you want to correct? Do certain things trigger "soapbox moments" for you? I had one of those at dinner recently. Another author was asking me about fibromyalgia and we got on the topic of the health care system. I realized after about 10 minutes that I was preaching loudly from my soapbox. It's easy for me to do the work that I do because I know I'm making a difference and I'm passionate about creating change—especially for chronically ill and pain patients. Find something that you're passionate about, and it will no longer be work.

On the application to join my training program, I ask each person why they want to become a Certified Fibromyalgia Coach or Advisor. Here are some quotes from applications I've received:

"I would love nothing more than to help other fibromyalgia patients, who are often treated horribly or treated very dismissively by their doctors."

"It has been a very long road to recovery, with so many ups and downs without any support. I have learned to manage but I know there is so much more to learn. But I want to do more than learn, I want to make a difference in other people's lives. I have such a strong desire to learn and help others and myself."

"I'm interested in helping other people who suffer from fibromyalgia. I'm personally affected by the disease. I'm fine today, but I want others to recover too! I feel it's my moral responsibility to help others who are where I used to be."

As I mentioned earlier, my sister was in her second year of veterinary medicine when she passed away. What I didn't say before is that she quit her full-time accounting job to go back to school to become a veterinarian. I remember when she made the decision. She realized that she looked forward to her "side job" more than her "real job." Several years earlier, she had started pet sitting for friends and co-workers. She built up quite a business and was in great demand. There were times she was at her clients' homes more than she was at her own! She ended up caring for mostly "special needs" pets. She gave shots, eye drops, medications, and I don't know what else. She realized that those things were a joy to her. She knew she was making a difference in both the lives of the pets and their owners, who both would stress out when traveling. As evidenced by her work with Pro-Bone-O, she was becoming a veterinarian to change the world in her own way.

How are you going to make a difference in the world?

 *Action Steps*

Take some time to consider your picture and definition of success. Do you want to make a lot of money? Or just contribute a little to your family's income? Do you want to change lives? Receive awards or accolades? Accomplish great things and leave a legacy? Do you want to be known as a volunteer with a heart of service, like my sister? What would make *you* feel like a success?

As always, start with awareness. If you're not sure how you define success, start paying attention to those times you feel successful. You can start your awareness campaign by looking at other areas of your life. Do you feel awesome when you clean out and organize a closet? Do you like volunteering? For what causes? Are you motivated by results and take pride in a job well done?

As a Mary Kay consultant, I worked hard to earn lots of little sparkly pieces of jewelry. They were things that probably cost my Sales Director just a few dollars. It would have been easier to just pay $3 for the item myself—but that wasn't the point. The point was being able to wear them to our sales meetings and have other people know what I accomplished. It was about *earning* them and about the recognition. Many people do the same thing at Weight Watchers meetings. The "bling," as my mom calls it, keeps some people motivated and makes them feel successful. If this is you, then public recognition and rewards might be important for you to include in your definition of success.

Maybe you would rather stay in the background, like my sister. One of the things that helped me enjoy her Celebration of Life is that she would have been mortified to have that much praise and attention focused on her... and as her ornery big sister, I loved being able to brag on her when she couldn't do anything about it. <grin>

Once you know what would make you feel fulfilled, take some time to consider the two key questions I discussed above, in light of whatever career you're considering. Will you receive a good return on your investment? Will you make the difference in the world that you want to make?

Chapter 7

Should You Be a Fibromyalgia Coach?

"Successful management of any chronic illness requires a large component of education on self-management skills. In an ideal world, every fibromyalgia patient's health care team would include a Fibromyalgia Coach or Advisor, along with a medical professional."

– Ginevra Liptan, MD

As you reviewed the eight key questions in the previous chapters, did you find anything that surprised you?

For me, all the answers pointed towards being some kind of coach. I needed to work with people—and from home where I could control my hours, deadlines, and environment. I needed to help people and make a difference in the world. I liked solving puzzles and helping people figure things out. With everything I had learned about managing my own fibromyalgia, coaching others through that journey seemed like a perfect way to allow the pain I suffered to count for something. I already had the skills and equipment necessary. I'd been informally coaching people my whole life. I decided to become a Certified Health Coach to strengthen my skills and fill in any gaps that I might have in my knowledge and experience.

What is a Fibromyalgia Coach?

A Fibromyalgia Coach (or Fibromyalgia Advisor) is someone specifically trained in how to manage fibromyalgia. We know the current science, treatment options, and lifestyle changes that will help your fibromyalgia symptoms improve. We have a network of providers we can refer you to who know how to treat fibromyalgia properly. Coaches and advisors are not doctors, so we can't diagnose or prescribe. However, we can often suggest tests or treatment options that you can discuss with your provider. We are also trained in how to help you implement the changes your doctor is recommending and can help you understand the tests, medications, and therapies your doctor has prescribed. We will also help you learn how to live with your illness in a way that allows you to thrive, not just survive.

I usually describe the work we do as being a cross between a life coach, a health coach, and a fibromyalgia educator. We aren't counselors, nor doctors, but we can help you understand your illness and thrive with it.

It wouldn't surprise me if you've never heard of a Fibromyalgia Coach. Years ago, when I started calling myself that, I'd never seen anyone else doing this kind of work. There may have been others out there, but I hadn't ever seen or met any. After my coaching practice became full, I discovered that I needed to duplicate myself. I hated having to tell people that I couldn't help them. (I still do!) In 2015, I founded the International Fibromyalgia Coaching Institute and began training new Fibromyalgia Coaches and Advisors. Even though this is a new career field, there are Certified Fibromyalgia Coaches and Advisors all over the world. To find one in your area, visit the Find a Coach page on the Institute website at FibromyalgiaCoachingInstitute.com.

What does a Fibromyalgia Coach do?

I described a bit of what we do in the section above, but it might be helpful for me to show you "a day in the life" of a Fibromyalgia Coach. As I'm writing this, I flipped open my calendar to a random week in 2015 and this is what it looks like:

- **Monday**—Two phone calls with clients; one 90-minute conference call with the Leaders Against Pain Action Network; miscellaneous administrative work, such as returning email, planning my week, and so on.
- **Tuesday**—Two hours at my BNI networking meeting, including mentoring new members; two phone calls with clients; administrative tasks.
- **Wednesday**—This is my self-care day, including lunch with a friend and a massage. Normally, Wednesdays are reserved for self-care and not working. However,

this particular week includes a two-hour conference call for the National Fibromyalgia & Chronic Pain Association's Chronic Pain Illness Education Support Guide committee.

- **Thursday**—Four phone calls with clients; miscellaneous administrative work.
- **Friday**—One phone call with a client; meeting with two providers (a chiropractor and a counselor) to learn more about their businesses and see how we can help each other with referrals.

The week described above was a pretty typical one for me. The amount of client calls and meetings with other people varies from week to week, but this gives you a pretty good idea. Weekends and evenings are personal time.

To recap, during the week described above, my Monday-Friday included:

- Working four days, generally between 10 AM - 6 PM
- Nine client calls
- Two conference calls
- Two meetings with other providers for referrals
- One networking meeting
- And a self-care day that included lunch with a friend and a massage

The nuts and bolts of being a Fibromyalgia Coach

I train my coaches and advisors to meet with their clients once a week for 45-60 minutes. This may vary depending on the client's needs. One of my clients moved across the country. During her move, we talked several times a week—there was just so much going on! Other clients, who might have less going on or who have fewer symptoms, I might meet with once a month. Still other clients have hired me for a specific purpose—to help them prepare for or recover from travel or a specific event.

I also recommend scheduling coaching calls at least 90 minutes apart. This allows 45 minutes for the client call, 15 minutes of wrap-up time to complete call notes and send any follow-up emails, and a 30-minute break. During my breaks, I get up, stretch, go to the bathroom, get a snack, refill my water bottle, rub The Belly of Happiness and Joy (aka, pet the cat), and do whatever self-care I need to keep feeling my best.

I do all my coaching over the phone. I decided right at the very beginning that I wanted to be able to meet with clients even if I was having a bad day—or if they were. I knew that meeting in person would be much harder for both of us. I also knew that if my client was having a bad day, she'd likely cancel her session if she had to meet in person—and that's when she would need me the most. I've also done some sessions by Skype or FaceTime. I had a client who was partially deaf and needed to read my lips while we were talking. Video is great for that!

I encourage the Fibromyalgia Coaches and Advisors I train to run their business in whatever way works best for them. Some work with their clients like I do, by phone. Others are doing video calls, meeting in person, teaching classes, and even running support groups in person and online.

Remember in an earlier chapter when I was telling you to make sure that you know what people *actually do* in a particular profession? Remember, when I told you that I decided not to be an interior designer because I thought that it meant shopping and working with people—but it really meant working alone on designs? Being a Fibromyalgia Coach or Advisor does mean working with people. It also means doing things like advertising, marketing, sales calls, building relationships with other providers to get referrals, doing your bookkeeping, answering email, returning phone calls, and all the other work involved in being the boss and running your own business. I do know a few coaches who are working as part of a clinic. However, this is the exception, not the norm. Most coaches still must find their own clients. I'll talk more about the challenges of this—and what you can do to make this easier—in the next chapter.

An unexpected bonus

I became a coach because I wanted to help people—and yes, to make a little money. But being a Fibromyalgia Coach gave me an unexpected bonus:

My fibromyalgia symptoms continue to improve. I keep feeling better and better!

The secret bonus of being a coach is that it keeps you on the straight and narrow, so to speak. Every day, I tell my clients things they can do to feel better. I remind them to get enough sleep, take their medications and supplements on schedule, eat in a way that helps them feel their best, manage their energy well, and so on. That means that every day, I hear myself and think, "Oh yes! I should do that too!" I'm continually reminded of *exactly* what I need to do to feel my best. Not only that, I either need to walk my talk, or I'm a hypocrite. Since I can't stand telling people to do things I'm not doing myself, it keeps me *doing* what I need to do, not just thinking about it.

When I first started my coaching business, I was in the middle of filing for Social Security disability. My plan was to coach a couple people and make a little extra money—but I definitely couldn't work full-time. In fact, I told my husband that *he* would have to do most of the coaching because I wasn't well enough. For those first few months, I sat in bed with my computer and my phone and coached my clients. Remember, I decided to work over the phone because I knew I was still having bad days here and there. I knew that no matter what, I could get on the phone for 45 minutes at a time and help my clients.

Six months after I started coaching, I was so much better that when I stood in front of a judge for my disability case, I no longer qualified. Today, I work full-time. I have zero body pain and enough energy to do the things I want to do. Nearly every month, I'm traveling for pleasure or business. This is something that wouldn't have been possible for me when I first started—and still wouldn't be possible if I wasn't a coach and always focused on my own healing. To be clear, there are still things I need to do to keep my symptoms under control. Most of the time, that's just good self-care, like getting enough sleep and managing my energy well. However, it can also include things like treatments and medications. It is important to remember that all these things are just tools. They are tools to help us feel our best once we know how to use them properly.

Answering the Eight Key Questions

Let's look at the eight key questions in relation to working as a Fibromyalgia Coach or Advisor:

1. How much control will I have over hours and deadlines?

There really aren't any deadlines with this kind of work. In many ways, there are no "coaching emergencies." Yes, there are times when a client might urgently need my help. But if it truly falls into the realm of "emergency," she probably needs to call emergency medical services or a counseling hotline, not me! I've designed my business so that there are no tasks left hanging after a client call. I've built in time after each call to do anything I need to do regarding that call. If I need to send the client information, make a provider referral or introduction, or anything else, I can do it as part of the wrap-up time built into my schedule. Returning email and phone calls are also built into my schedule, stated on my voice mail, and blocked out on my calendar.

As for work hours, it depends on how you choose to do your work. If you are like most coaches and advisors, you will be able to set your own hours. If you are working out of a clinic, you may be limited to the clinic's hours.

One thing to keep in mind is who you want to work with. If your ideal client is a young working adult, you may need to offer appointments after work or during lunch times. If you're wanting to work with moms of teenagers, they may need appointments when their kids are at school. Time zones can work for or against you here. I'm in Oregon, so I'm on Pacific time. I work from 10 AM to 6 PM, but that's 1-9 PM Eastern time. I often work with clients on the east coast after their work hours, but only have a couple appointments a week for local clients after 5 PM.

2. What equipment or skill set will I need?

In terms of equipment, this depends on how you choose to run your business and what works best for you. You can do this job with almost nothing. When I started out as a coach, I used what I already had. I didn't buy anything new. I used the computer, phone, and headset I already had. I set up a free email account through Google. I used text editing software that came with my computer for keeping track of customer records.

Over the years I've added things like online appointment scheduling software, a separate phone and fax line for business, and so on. I tried fancy customer management software but found that it wasn't as useful to me as a text editor and my calendar. I've also added things like a website, blog, Facebook page, business cards, fliers, brochures, and so on—but these were added *after* I started working with clients. You might wonder where those first clients came from if I didn't have a website, business cards, or brochures. The answer is direct outreach—me reaching out to people I know, telling them what I do and who I can help, and offering to help them. Most of my business still finds me this way.

As far as skills are concerned, there isn't anything you need to know before joining my training and certification program. I will teach you what you need to know. However, there are two skills I can't teach you. These are the only two things I look for when I'm interviewing potential new coaches. Those two things are:

- A genuine desire to help people. If you're not good with people, or if you want to make money *more* than you want to help others, it will be hard to be a good coach. (BTW—If you want to make money, that's totally okay! I just want to make sure that your focus is on loving people and helping them. Ironically, you'll also make more money if you have a heart of service.)

- A desire to do things correctly. Since we are talking about people's health, it's super important for me to train people who want to do things correctly. I need to know that they are going to advise their clients in a way that will help and not harm. They need to be able to pay attention to the details.

If you choose to go your own route in becoming a Fibromyalgia Coach or Advisor, then you'll need to learn and keep up-to-date with the things I teach in my training and certification program:

- Current fibromyalgia science and research
- Medications and treatment plans
- Natural alternatives for fibromyalgia medications
- Complementary and integrative therapies that work for fibromyalgia

- Comorbid conditions and how they impact fibromyalgia
- How to reduce pain, increase energy, and get better sleep
- Pacing and energy management
- Fibromyalgia-specific nutrition and exercise plans
- Gentle goal-setting and action planning
- Stress management strategies
- Self-care and coping techniques
- How to work with doctors and other providers
- Testifying for client disability cases
- Developing your ideal client profile
- How fibromyalgia coaching differs from other coaching practices
- Developing a network of trusted providers

You may also need to learn skills related to running your business, or you may choose to have someone do these things for you. For example, you may need to learn about:

- Conducting sales calls
- Bookkeeping
- Record keeping for taxes
- Advertising
- Networking
- Social media
- Branding
- And so on

3. What is the volume of work?

Remember that there are two ways to answer this question. First, what is the *potential* volume of work? Are there enough people out there who need a Fibromyalgia Coach or Advisor? Absolutely! There is a huge need, with three to six percent of the world's population being diagnosed with fibromyalgia. Just in the United States alone, that's 9.5 to 19 million people.

In terms of how much work you will do yourself, you absolutely get to choose. You can decide how many hours you want to work—and can vary those hours depending on your needs.

4. Is being a Fibromyalgia Coach or Advisor physically demanding?

Not very demanding at all. There are a lot of variables you can play with to make it fit your needs. For example, you can use a headset or do video calls instead of holding a phone to your ear. You can choose to work from bed or a standing desk, or from a zero-gravity chair and lap desk, like I do. You can type, handwrite, or dictate your client call notes. You can do one client session a day, one a week, or one an hour. You have total control over this.

5. How mentally demanding is it to be a Fibromyalgia Coach or Advisor?

Working with clients can be mentally demanding—but only for about 45 minutes at a time. If you naturally have the people skills I mentioned in question two, then this should be fairly easy. You also have the ability to switch up the way you coach, since you would be your own boss. For example, if you can only focus for 20 minutes at a time, you could structure your coaching business around 20-minute calls. I did this with a client who was recovering from a stroke. Since the client could only focus for that long, we did two 20-minute sessions a week instead of one a week for 45 minutes.

I find that the biggest "mental muscles" I use as a coach are my problem-solving skills. If a client is struggling with a particular symptom, didn't meet her goal, or has another challenge come up, I always troubleshoot the issue with her and help her come up with a creative solution. Sometimes this requires thinking outside the box, but it always requires *thinking*. Being a coach is not mindless work. However, if you're a people person or an extrovert, this kind of work can be stimulating, not draining.

It's important to remember that it's totally okay to say, "I don't know. Let me check into that and get back to you." I stress with all my students that it's most important to know *how to find* the information you need. I know what it's like to deal with brain fog. When fibro brain strikes, it can be hard to recall information you know that you know. When I coach, I'm continually searching my computer and the Internet. I know I have anything my client needs at my fingertips, even if I can't remember it without help.

6. *How social is a Fibromyalgia Coach's job?*

You can't be a coach and not work with people. This is social work. However, you do have flexibility over how social it is. For example, you could choose to work with people in groups or one-on-one. You could choose to do your coaching sessions over the phone or in person. You could choose to do a bunch of client calls back-to-back, or space them out. You could have one client or many. All of these things will affect how social the work is for you. If you'd rather not talk to people, however, being a coach probably isn't for you!

7. *Will I get a good return on my investment of time, energy, and money as a Fibromyalgia Coach?*

I think the answer is *absolutely!*

Being a coach has paid me back far more than it has taken from me. As I mentioned earlier, my own fibromyalgia has improved to the point it's no longer a factor for me. I don't have body pain. I have enough energy to do the things I want to do. I am in control of my body and my life. The energy and time I put into coaching is returned to me multiplied as my health and energy levels have improved. Helping my clients gets me excited and jazzed up, which gives me more energy.

I guarantee that if you follow the things you learn on your journey to becoming a Fibromyalgia Coach, your fibromyalgia symptoms will improve as well. You'll be learning about treatments, medications, supplements, and other therapies that work. You'll know how to manage your energy and improve your sleep. You'll learn how to make choices that support your healing instead of sending you into a fibro flare. A recent graduate told me that she took the class because she wanted to help others, but was surprised that her own fibromyalgia improved. She said, "This class has changed *everything* for me!" I know that she would agree, the return on investment is excellent.

The return on the money investment has also been fantastic. When I started out, I made the choice to invest most of what I made back into my business in the form of additional training, education, advertising, coaching, and more. (Yes, even coaches need to have a coach!) The result of that investment is that I make more money working for myself than I ever did working for someone else.

Most likely, if you choose to become a Fibromyalgia Coach or Advisor, you will need to make an investment of money, in addition to your time and energy. If you invest in the right things along your journey, it will pay off for you. Do your due diligence and make sure that what you're investing in will provide the results you're after.

As you start looking, you'll find that there are a lot of good life and health coaching certification programs out there. The cost on these range from a few hundred to many thousands of dollars over the course of a few months to several years. Depending on your experience, what you need, and what you want to do when you're done, some programs will be better for you than others. My training and certification program teaches the fibromyalgia piece of things. Other programs don't talk about fibromyalgia at all, but cover more general health, psychology, and coaching than I do. If you're wondering which route is the best one for you, let's talk. I'd love to help you get clear on what your next step should be and what the best investment is for you. You can contact me through the Institute website at FibromyalgiaCoachingInstitute.com.

8. Will I be making a difference as a Fibromyalgia Coach?

ABSOLUTELY.

The only way to not make a difference is to never work with anyone or apply what you learn to your own life. I have several students who have graduated and haven't worked with a single client. They are still making a difference because their own lives are improving. This means that they can do more for their kids, grandkids, or parents. They are more involved in their communities (in person and online) and are changing lives in other ways.

As a coach, I get messages nearly every day about how I'm making a difference for the people around me. I just took a few minutes to look in my inbox. Here are quotes from two emails that are sitting in my box as I write:

> *"I came across your website quite by accident through Pinterest and was happy to see that I wasn't the only one feeling this way. I was diagnosed with fibromyalgia in 2009 more or less. Everything I read in your article describes me to a T. Maybe there is hope after all."*

> *"I'm enjoying your book so far; it is the second one I have begun reading on fibromyalgia since my doctor said I might have it. I like your book better and am glad*

it is written by someone who has been there. Thank you for writing it and having a blog and a newsletter. You are great!"

I could tell you about making a difference, or you could read about it in my clients' own words:

"Thank you so, so much. You helped me find [my doctor] and it changed my life. Prior to seeing her I was seeing an arthritis doctor who wouldn't listen to me. I was in so much pain day to day I was bed bound. I have a small child and it was daunting. So, thank you."—Kim

"Each month, I've seen that my [bad] days are becoming fewer and fewer… I really like being able to go on dates with my husband again. It has been SO long since we were able to go on dates, and now we're able to do that. And it's awesome!"—Laura

"I literally couldn't move off the couch. Now I can do things in the evening!"—Tania

I've also received a handful of messages from people who told me that meeting me literally saved their lives, like this one I received just recently:

"I just wanted you to know that your videos have helped me more than you could ever imagine… Thank you for saving my life when I was ready to just not be alive anymore."

So many people message me to say that they were hurting and without hope. They were contemplating suicide as a way to end their misery. Meeting me was the thing that kept them from giving up on life.

Talk about making a difference!

 *Action Steps*

Review the answers you wrote down for these eight key questions and compare them to what it's like to work as a Fibromyalgia Coach. Is it clear to you if this would be a good fit for you, your needs, and your goals?

If you're stuck on "maybe," let's talk. I would be happy to give you whatever information you need for you to get clear on if it's "yes" or "no." I would also recommend visiting FibromyalgiaCoachingInstitute.com to learn about the training program, read stories about our graduates, and listen to our virtual graduations and open house events.

We should also talk if it's already a clear "Yes!" I would love to help you figure out what your next step should be—whether it's learning from me, on your own, or joining another training program. If you know you want to help people in this way, you don't have to wait until you know it all. You can help people around you just by listening and being there for them. You can start doing that right now.

Chapter 8

Common Obstacles to Success

"There are many obstacles in your path.
Don't allow yourself to become one of them."
–Ralph Marston

"The road to success is dotted
with many tempting parking spots."
– Will Rogers

O n your journey to find a career that will support your health—and even encourage healing—you will encounter obstacles. There will be times you want to give up or even feel that you *must* give up. Instead, I invite you to consider those times as learning moments.

I truly believe that wherever you are is *exactly* where you're supposed to be. Most people believe in something that says there's an opportunity to learn from this moment and this challenge. Maybe they call it karma, the law of attraction, or the process of evolution. I believe it's the providence of God. I believe that it's our response to these challenges that makes us who we are and defines our lives.

I know you'll think I'm crazy, but I am honest-to-God thankful for my fibromyalgia. A friend posted on Facebook the other day and asked her friends to share their "unpopular opinions." This is mine: *I truly love my fibromyalgia.* Fibromyalgia has given me so much more than it's taken away. I have a new and better life. I am a better person now than I was before I was living intimately with fibromyalgia. I get to help more people and make a bigger difference in the world than I ever would have if I hadn't developed fibromyalgia.

Without fibromyalgia, it would be easy for me to fall back into my old habits of putting myself last and running my body into the ground. Thanks to fibromyalgia, I'm super in-tune with my body. I know right away if something isn't right physically.

I was discussing listening to our bodies with my sister after she was diagnosed with cancer. We were talking about the signs her body had given her that something was wrong. She hadn't recognized them for what they were, and they didn't find her cancer until it was too late. I will tell you the same thing I told her—there's nothing you can do about the past. You can't change the fact that maybe you haven't listened to your body as well as you could have. But you *can* change what you do from this point forward. Allow fibromyalgia to be your friend and your guide. There are many treasures to discover in these learning opportunities!

Let's take a moment to talk about a few of the common obstacles to finding your perfect fibro-friendly career. No matter what career you choose, you will likely come across these challenges. I've included below how I've dealt with them myself, and what I teach the coaches and advisors in my training program.

I don't have any training—or don't have the right training.

If I haven't already, I'll just lay it all on the table right here. I didn't graduate from high school or college. I was a smart kid in a small town and bored out of my mind. I took a high school equivalency exam and moved on. When I got to college, I discovered that I didn't know what I wanted to do with my life, and college tuition was too expensive to waste on playing around. At that point, I left college and started working.

However, *I love to learn!* This has led me to take many online and in-person training programs. Topics have covered a wide range of subjects, such as personal development, sales, management, coaching, treating chronic pain, writing, math, even art and Photoshop! (I'll admit that I took a college algebra class *just for fun!*)

I use things every day while I'm coaching that have come from every job I've ever had. That includes things like:

- my sales and skin care training as a Mary Kay consultant
- how to track conversations and call notes from my time working with in-warranty repairs at a TV repair shop
- listening for the "question behind the question" when I provided tech support for a software company
- public speaking from my time as a tour guide at Undersea Gardens
- graphic design skills I developed working with my dad's art business, Acrewood Art
- marketing, copywriting, training, and general business management from being a Customer Service Manager

Maybe you've had a wild work background like I have. I guarantee you that there are things to learn and use from *every job* that you've had. Although I don't often get to use my skills in working with sea lions, I do use many of the other things I learned at Undersea Gardens.

Once you've found your answers to the eight key questions presented earlier in this book, and you know what career you want to pursue, you can absolutely find ways to get the training you need to augment the skills you already have. If you're interested in becoming a Fibromyalgia Coach or Advisor, I offer a training program to teach you everything you need to know about working with fibromyalgia patients. If you want to be a graphic designer, there are classes you can take at your local community college or online. Search out and find whatever it is that you need.

It is never too late to pursue the career of your dreams. You may have read the dedication at the front of this book. In case you don't remember, this book is dedicated to my sister, Debbi, because she was brave enough to give up a successful full-time accounting career to move back in with our parents, rack up loads of student debt, and go back to school for seven more years to follow her dream to be a veterinarian. I want you to know that she quit her accounting job when she was 36. She started vet school at 40. I also want you to know that *while she was undergoing cancer treatment, she signed up for fall classes.* She never gave up, even when she was sick. It's never too late, no matter your age or your health. Even though my sister didn't graduate before cancer took her life, I would still say it wasn't too late. Too late would have been facing cancer knowing she hadn't even started working towards her dream. She died in pursuit of her dream and her last few years were her happiest.

As a practical side note, no matter what business you want to get into, there will most likely be classes you can take online. I think online classes are a bit easier for those of us with fibromyalgia. However, a woman in my support group went back to school at one of the local universities. She received many accommodations that made it easier for her to attend. She received a pass for parking spaces close to her classes. The school held her classes on the first floor of the building—or in rooms that were accessible to her scooter via elevator. She also received accommodations for test taking, extra time in completing certain assignments, and so on.

There are ways to get the training you need, even with fibromyalgia.

Where and how will I find clients?

First off, let me say that no matter what career you choose, unless you're working for someone else who does the sales and marketing, you *will* need to find clients.

Some people just don't like sales and marketing. These people often decide that they would rather work for someone else than own their own businesses. I have a good friend who is a fantastic trainer. In fact, she's the one who taught me nearly everything I know about how to network with other businesses. As fantastic as she was, owning her own business was stressful for her. She found that she avoided doing the work necessary to find clients. She decided that what would make her happiest would be to work for someone else, who would find and send clients to her. That way she could focus on the part she loved—training others.

If you want to work for yourself, there are ways to find clients more easily. This is a question I am asked by nearly every student. Therefore, I have included this training as part of my program.

To receive their certifications, my students are required to prepare an ideal client profile. This is something that usually takes a few rounds of feedback before I approve it. Most people don't get this right on the first try. I certainly didn't! Like many health coaches, I thought I could help "anyone who wanted better health." It wasn't until I spoke with my first fibromyalgia client that I understood the power of what I had to offer. I could help her so much more, because of my own life experiences. She received more out of the coaching call, because she was connecting with someone who *truly understood* for the first time, maybe ever. When I hung up the phone after that first call, I felt like the universe was revolving around me. It was a "burning bush moment." I am being completely sincere when I tell you: *I felt like I needed to remove my shoes and kneel on the ground because this was a holy moment.* I felt like Esther who was, "born for such a time as this."

When you work with your "just right" people, everything will change. The work will be easy, not hard. You will create all kinds of breakthroughs for your clients. You will start to change lives. Because of their results, your clients will become raving fans, telling everyone they can about you. Your clients' doctors will see how much better they are doing and will want all their patients to work with you. When you are clear about your ideal client, it's almost as if you become a magnet that draws your clients to you.

As my friend Cassie Parks says on her *Happy Ever After* podcast, "I am a lighthouse, not a tugboat." Selling your services will be difficult if you're trying to "tugboat" people. Not to mention the fact that it just feels icky to try to convince someone to buy something from you. It's also icky to be on the receiving end of that too, right?

However, when you are crystal clear about who your ideal client is, and clear about the life you want to live, that clarity will shine out of you like a lighthouse beacon. Not only will you know your ideal client well enough to know exactly where she hangs out, your perfect people will be able to find you, like a ship seeing a lighthouse in the dark. It feels so much better to have people say, "I want what you have to offer. How can I work with you?" It's like the movie *When Harry Met Sally*. This is the "I'll have what she's having!" moment.

Another thing I teach in my training program is how to connect with other providers for referrals. As a Fibromyalgia Coach, nearly all my clients come to me through referrals—from clients, my support group, other providers, and so on.

In some ways, developing referral relationships with doctors and providers is the same as developing any other referral relationship. Like all relationships, it requires nurturing. Out of sight many times means out of mind. If you're not getting referrals, it might be because you need to develop the relationship and take it deeper. Think of this like dating. You (probably) wouldn't have sex on the first date. Likewise, don't ask for referrals the first time you meet with someone! They will need to get to know you and trust you before they will hand over their clients to you. Heck, they need to know if they even *like* you or not!

Where doctors and providers differ from other referral sources is in how you need to develop the relationship. It might be challenging to have a "coffee date" with a doctor. Their day is usually full of back-to-back patient appointments—which doesn't leave much time for visiting with someone who is asking you for referrals. And when I put it that way, doesn't it feel just a little bit icky? We often go in with an attitude of, "Please take some time out of your busy schedule to help me build MY business." Yuck! No wonder it's usually not successful! Trust me, I've made this mistake myself. I remember talking to my doctor when I first became a coach. I told her, "I would love to help any of your other fibromyalgia patients." She politely declined.

The result was totally my fault because of how I approached the situation. I was asking her to grow my business. Remember when I was talking about having a heart of service earlier? The same thing goes for building relationships with providers.

Whatever career you choose, you will likely need to develop referral relationships. Asentiv (formerly The Referral Institute) and BNI (Business Network International) are two organizations I recommend for learning how to develop referral relationships.

What if I'm having a bad day? My health isn't predictable yet.

Now we're getting to the *real* concerns you have about working, right? It's something we don't like to talk about, but this is the real deal right here. It's why we suspect that our employers aren't happy with our work. Some days we're rock stars; other days we are exhausted masses of pain that can't think. What do you do?

First, be honest with yourself about where you are at *right now*. The eight key questions I've given you in earlier chapters should help you do this. Perhaps you've discovered that you do your best work in the late afternoon and evening. Or that you can only concentrate for an hour at a time. Or that staring at a computer screen for hours on end gives you a migraine. The first step is always becoming aware. If you don't know what you need, you're stuck. Once you know, you can do something about changing your situation.

Second, begin creating a work environment that supports the needs you've identified using the eight key questions I've given you. Creating your perfect work environment might mean talking with your boss. Or it might mean finding something new altogether.

In my case, I've structured my business and my work environment so that I can feel my best and do my best work. This means I'm only on the phone for 45 minutes to an hour at a time, then I have a break. I often work from my zero-gravity recliner with a headset and my laptop. I take a day off in the middle of the week, which means I only work two days in a row. I don't start work before 10 AM and am done by 6 PM. I only work with clients and providers that I enjoy and genuinely like being around. I'm never on the computer too long. Even as I'm writing this book, I'm using the Pomodoro Technique, a system of working and resting. I work for 25 minutes, rest for five minutes, with longer breaks as needed. You can learn more on their website: PomodoroTechnique.com.

All this means that I rarely have bad days. As I've mentioned earlier in this book, however, there were many days I coached from my bed when I started. That was how I dealt with bad days. Yes, I have occasionally had to cancel appointments. In fact, as I was writing this book, I cancelled one of my classes because I was exhausted from my husband being in the hospital all week for gallbladder surgery. It happens sometimes—*to all of us*. The great thing about the work I do is that my clients totally get it! After all, they have fibromyalgia and bad days too. Often, if I cancel or rearrange something, the replies I get are telling me to take care of myself. I don't think I've ever received a reply from someone who was mad. Ever. I can't say the same for the bosses I've had when I called in sick for work!

In my training program, I help my students plan for a successful business. One of their required assignments is to fill out the Dream Week Planner for when they are working with clients. Some have had to create more than one plan. Sometimes, I give them feedback that what they've planned isn't realistic for their particular health situation. Other times they need more than one plan because they are transitioning out of one career into another. If you're already working a full-time job and want to transition to something more fibro-friendly, you may need to create a plan for your transition, not just a plan for the ultimate goal. If you're interested in using the Dream Week Planner to plan your best work schedule, you can find the worksheet on my website at FibromyalgiaCoachingInstitute.com/book-bonuses. Detailed directions on using this worksheet are also found in my first book, *Take Back Your Life,* in the chapter titled, "How Can I Have More Energy?"

The bottom line on having bad days or being unpredictable is two-fold: 1) Plan your work schedule so that you have the best possible chance of success, and 2) know that your clients will understand if you need to change something.

How can I help others if my own fibromyalgia isn't under control yet?

This question is slightly different from the last one and applies more specifically to working as a Fibromyalgia Coach or Advisor. For many people, this is like wanting to be a weight loss coach and still being overweight yourself. You might think that you don't have anything to offer and that you can't help anyone yet.

But think about it this way instead....

If you wanted to lose weight, who would you rather get advice from? The girl who was skinny, and never had to struggle with her weight? Or the person who was 50 pounds overweight but had already lost 50 pounds?

I'd absolutely choose the one who understood my struggle best—the one who isn't there yet, but who has already had some success. Wouldn't you?

Fibromyalgia clients are the exact same way. You only need to be a little bit further ahead of them on the journey. You know how frustrating it is to go to a doctor or talk to a friend who completely doesn't get it—because they've never struggled with fibromyalgia themselves. There is so much healing in simply talking with someone who understands. Sometimes, that's all a client needs—someone to listen and say, "I understand. I've been there too."

You can help other people simply by listening and understanding.

Remember that secret gift that being a Fibromyalgia Coach has given me? *My own symptoms improved because I was helping others.*

I can't offer you a 100% satisfaction guarantee on your fibromyalgia magically improving just by being a coach. Obviously, there's more to it than that. Here is what I can promise you: If you learn all the things I teach in my training program and implement them in your own life, it's almost impossible to *not* improve. Do you know what's in this program? It's all the things I learned when I was working on improving my own health. It's all the things I've found that help my clients. It's all the stuff I know that *works*. If you learn all the same stuff I have—and use what you learn—you can't help but feel better!

To be clear, there are other ways to learn this information besides taking my training program. After all, I didn't! I learned all of this over the last 25+ years working with clients, reading everything I could get my hands on, going to training conferences, listening to doctor lectures, reading research studies, asking questions, and trying things out on myself. You can totally do that yourself. All the info is out there for you to find. All I've done is combine the things I found to be most helpful into one place to make it as easy and as fast as possible for you.

The other thing I want to say about helping others is this: You will always help more people by just *trying to help people* than you will by waiting until you're perfect.

As I was working on my first book, I used this quote by Jon Acuff to keep me motivated, "90 percent perfect and shared with the world always changes more lives than 100 percent perfect and stuck in your head."

There are people out there who cry themselves to sleep at night because they can't find someone to help them. For some, *you are the only person who can help them,* because of your individual life experiences, knowledge, and personality. Those people don't care if you're overweight. They don't care if your dishes are in the sink or that you ordered takeout because it was the only way you could manage dinner tonight. They don't care if your kids aren't perfect or you sometimes argue with your husband. All they want is someone who can come alongside them, listen to them, care about them, and give them an idea of how to get through the next day.

Here's the deal—you can tell them exactly what I just told you. This is from my heart and *my real life* to yours, in all honesty and transparency:

Don't worry about being overweight. I am too. Don't worry about the dirty dishes in the sink. Mine aren't done either. It's okay to order takeout when you're busy. That's what I did for dinner tonight. Don't worry about having perfect kids or a perfect marriage. You must take care of yourself first so that you can teach your family how you want to be treated. You can feel better. Let me show you how.

Conclusion

As I said at the beginning, my goal for this book is two-fold.

First and foremost, I want to provide you, as a fibromyalgia patient, a way to evaluate your needs so that you can find the best job *for you*. My goal is that the information I've provided here will help you as much as it has helped me and my clients.

Using the answers from the eight key questions in this book, you can begin to create your ideal work environment. You can assess and address your physical needs, your mental and social needs, and measure your success. You can begin to plan for common challenges and obstacles that may come up for you. Most importantly, I hope you now realize that you already have a full-time job. One that is more important than any other job you will ever find—*healing*.

My second goal is to provide enough information on what a Fibromyalgia Coach is and does that you will know if being a coach or working with a coach might be helpful for you. You can connect with one of my Certified Fibromyalgia Coaches and Advisors at FibromyalgiaCoachingInstitute.com.

There are so many more people out there than I can help on my own—and I have a dream. A big dream.

My dream is that someday fibromyalgia patients all over the world will have a choice in who they partner with to find their healing. I dream of a day when teenagers with fibromyalgia will have someone they can work with who understands the unique challenges they face when doctors tell them they are too young to hurt that much. I dream of a day when men with fibromyalgia can work with a male coach who understands the internal conflict of being a "tough guy" or "the provider of the family" when you're in constant pain. I dream of a world where it's easy for patients to find a Fibromyalgia Coach or Advisor who speaks their own language, understands their culture and customs, and can help them navigate their country's health care system. I want moms with fibromyalgia to be able to have a coach who knows what it's like to feel like they have to choose between taking care of themselves or taking care of their kids. I want young adults to work with a coach who knows the frustration of staying home when they're too tired to go out dancing with their friends. I want career women to have someone who can help them navigate how to talk with their bosses and co-workers about their fibromyalgia.

I can't do all of this on my own, which is why I'm so excited to be training new Fibromyalgia Coaches and Advisors. Together, we can change the world—one fibromyalgia patient at a time!

Endnotes

1. National Fibromyalgia & Chronic Pain Association. Fibromyalgia Fact Sheet. 10 Feb 2016. Web. 12 Jan 2017. https://www.fibroandpain.org/fibromyalgia/fm-fact-sheet

2. Rheumatology.org. "Shortage of Rheumatologists–In Some U.S. Regions Closest Doctor May Be 200 Miles Away." 6 Nov 2013. Web. 12 Jan 2017. http://www.rheumatology.org/About-Us/Newsroom/Press-Releases/ID/29/Shortage-of-RheumatologistsIn-Some-US-Regions-Closest-Doctor-May-Be-200-Miles-Away

3. Rheumatology.org. "Shortage of Rheumatologists–In Some U.S. Regions Closest Doctor May Be 200 Miles Away." 6 Nov 2013. Web. 12 Jan 2017. http://www.rheumatology.org/About-Us/Newsroom/Press-Releases/ID/29/Shortage-of-RheumatologistsIn-

Some-US-Regions-Closest-Doctor-May-Be-200-Miles-Away

4. Michael E. Schatman, PhD, CPE. "Who Really Treats Chronic Pain? The Necessity of Pain Management in Family Practice." MD Magazine. 21 Apr 2014. Web. 12 Jan 2017. http://www.hcplive.com/journals/family-practice-recertification/2014/april2014/who-really-treats-chronic-pain-the-necessity-of-pain-management-in-family-practice

5. Michael E. Schatman, PhD, CPE. "Who Really Treats Chronic Pain? The Necessity of Pain Management in Family Practice." MD Magazine. 21 Apr 2014. Web. 12 Jan 2017. http://www.hcplive.com/journals/family-practice-recertification/2014/april2014/who-really-treats-chronic-pain-the-necessity-of-pain-management-in-family-practice

6. National Ambulatory Medical Care Survey: 2010 Summary Tables. Centers for Disease Control and Prevention. Web. 12 Jan 2017. http://www.cdc.gov/nchs/data/ahcd/namcs_summary/2010_namcs_web_tables.pdf

7. Rabin, Roni Caryn. 15-Minute Visits Take A Toll On The Doctor-Patient Relationship. Kaiser Health News. 21 Apr 2014. Web. 12 Jan 2017. http://kaiserhealthnews.org/news/15-minute-doctor-visits/

8. McGonigal, Kelly. How to Make Stress Your Friend. TED. Sep 2013. Web. 12 Jan 2017. http://www.ted.com/talks/kelly_mcgonigal_how_to_make_stress_your_friend

9. Bennett, Robert M et al. "An Internet Survey of 2,596 People with Fibromyalgia." BMC Musculoskeletal Disorders 8 (2007): 27. PMC. Web. 12 Jan. 2017. http://www.ncbi.nlm.nih.gov/pmc/articles/PMC1829161

10. Thompson, Jeffrey M., et al. "Direct medical costs in patients with fibromyalgia: cost of illness and impact of a brief multidisciplinary treatment program." American Journal of Physical Medicine & Rehabilitation 90.1 (2011): 40-46.

11. Harker, K. Troy, et al. "Exploring attentional disruption in fibromyalgia using the attentional blink." Psychology & health 26.7 (2011): 915-929.

Acknowledgments

Thank you to…

Fibromyalgia. You gave me a new life once I stopped fighting the lessons you were trying to teach me. It took a while, but I'm so thankful we're friends.

Alumni of the International Fibromyalgia Coaching Institute. I am so proud to have each of you working alongside me. I am particularly grateful to Brenda Faverio, Cindy Sharp, Emma Christensen, Julie Hamilton, Kate Straus, Laura Holcomb, Mary Jaeger, Melissa Swanson, Rebecca Sinkule, Sandra Meza, Simone Cohn, Tamie Galbreath, and Terry McSweeney, who trusted me enough to sign up for my very first class while it was just a dream and a twinkle in my eye. These women, along with the students and graduates around the world who have joined them, were brave enough to become Certified Fibromyalgia Coaches and Advisors when it wasn't even a thing yet. It takes a lot of courage to be on the cutting edge of a new career field. I didn't expect how much I would learn from each of you in return! You know we're stuck together for life, right?

Angela Lauria, Maggie McReynolds, and my fellow authors at Difference Press. None of us change the world alone. Thank you for seeing me as I can be, not as I always feel like I am. You have held my dreams for the future, even when I've forgotten them or feel like they're too big to hold on my own. Thank you, Maggie, for standing in so well for my ideal reader and helping me see this book through her eyes. Out of all the things you did for me as my editor, that was the one that helped the most. I especially thank you, Angela, for kicking my butt when I needed it. Without your tough love, I wouldn't be here. You never let me take the easy way out and accepted me into an amazing group of authors and coaches that give me something to aspire to.

To the Morgan James Publishing team. Special thanks to David Hancock, CEO & Founder for believing in me and my message. To my Author Relations Manager, Margo Toulouse, thanks for making the process seamless and easy. Many more thanks to everyone else, but especially Jim Howard, Bethany Marshall, and Nickcole Watkins. I love that fibromyalgia has touched some of you and that you understand why I'm so passionate about what I do.

Mom and Dad. I wouldn't be where I am if you hadn't given me space to find my own way. My calling ended up being much different than any of us expected. It's also been so much more awesome!

My husband, Scott. Thank you for allowing me to pursue the full-time job that was dumped into my lap when I was diagnosed with fibromyalgia (my healing). You didn't sign up to be married to someone who was sick. I know there were times it was scary and confusing. Thanks for sticking by me. I couldn't have gotten better without your support.

My sister, Debbi. I choose to believe that you can read this even from heaven. Thanks for always being the brave sister who would go first, even though I'm older. You were always so much braver than me. This is a different book because of the journey I took with you this year.

The Great Storyteller. You always tell redemption stories. Always. Even with fibromyalgia. Even with cancer. Even through death.

About the Author

 Tami Stackelhouse encourages hope and healing as a coach, author, speaker, and founder of the International Fibromyalgia Coaching Institute. A fibromyalgia patient herself, Tami has gone from disabled to thriving. Her compassion, gentle support, and fun coaching style help women with fibromyalgia take back control of their lives.

A Certified Health Coach and member of the Leaders Against Pain Action Network, Tami is the author of the bestselling book *Take Back Your Life: Find Hope and Freedom from Fibromyalgia Symptoms and Pain* (Difference Press, 2015). She has served as a panelist, instructor, presenter, and writer for organizations such as the National Fibromyalgia & Chronic Pain Association (NFCPA), Oregon Health & Science University, The Frida Center for Fibromyalgia, Oregon Fibromyalgia

Information Foundation, and Molly's Fund Fighting Lupus. She co-founded the Fibromyalgia-ME/CFS Support Center, Inc., a nonprofit support community, and served as their Vice President from 2011 to 2015. In 2017, she founded the Sherri Little Foundation, a non-profit organization that will provide grants to chronic pain patients. She also serves as a mentor for the FibroAcademy support group.

As a patient advocate, Tami began working closely with the NFCPA and Oregon doctors in 2013 to petition policymakers to move fibromyalgia onto the Prioritized List of conditions covered by Medicaid reimbursement. As of 2017, that battle is still ongoing. Oregon remains the only state in the US that does not cover fibromyalgia treatment on their state health plan.

Tami lives in the suburbs of Portland, Oregon, with her husband, Scott, and their three cats: Sam, Jesse, and Sniglets. On sunny days, you'll find her on the back of Scott's Harley. When it's raining, she will be by the fire, reading a good book, and rubbing Sam's big Belly of Happiness and Joy.

Website: FibromyalgiaCoachingInstitute.com
Facebook: Facebook.com/FibroCoach
Twitter: Twitter.com/FibroCoach

Thank You

If you've read this far, THANK YOU! I'm always one to read all the acknowledgements in a book or liner notes—but I know everyone doesn't. I appreciate you sticking with me this far!

Throughout this book, I've mentioned several worksheets and exercises, such as the Dream Week Planner and the eight key questions worksheet. I also mentioned the special "Healing is a full-time job" mantra coloring page designed for this book by artist Anne Manera. You can download these goodies and more from my website at FibromyalgiaCoachingInstitute.com/book-bonuses.

There is also a Find a Coach page on that site that will help you connect to the Certified Fibromyalgia Coaches and Advisors in your area. I hope that you will take advantage of a free consultation with one of them to learn more about how they can help you feel better and get your life back.

If you already know that you want to become a Fibromyalgia Coach or Advisor, I would love talk with you to help you figure out what your next step should be—whether it's learning from me, on your own, or joining another training program. Visit FibromyalgiaCoachingInstitute.com to fill out a program application or schedule a call.

I would also love to talk with you if you're stuck on "maybe." I would be happy to give you whatever information you need to move from "maybe" to a clear "yes" or "no." I would also recommend visiting the Institute website to learn more about the training program, read stories about our graduates, and listen to one of our virtual graduations or open house events.

Become a Certified
Fibromyalgia Coach

and help others find hope
and freedom from fibromyalgia
symptoms and pain

*Our program includes
both live and self-paced study,
one-on-one mentoring, and a
coaching practicum*

learn more at
IFCINSTITUTE.COM

Morgan James
Speakers Group

We connect Morgan James published
authors with live and online events
and audiences who will benefit
from their expertise.

Morgan James makes all of our titles available
through the Library for All Charity Organization.

www.LibraryForAll.org